Simply Serge Any Fabric

Other books in the Creative Machine Arts Series, available from Chilton:

Claire Shaeffer's Fabric Sewing Guide

The Complete Book of Machine Embroidery, by Robbie and Tony Fanning

Creative Nurseries Illustrated, by Debra Terry and Juli Plooster

Creative Serging Illustrated, by Pati Palmer, Gail Brown and Sue Green

The Expectant Mother's Wardrobe Planner, by Rebecca Dumlao

The Fabric Lover's Scrapbook, by Margaret Dittman

Friendship Quilts by Hand and Machine, by Carolyn Vosburg Hall

Innovative Serging and *Innovative Sewing*, by Gail Brown and Tammy Young

Know Your Bernina, by Jackie Dodson

Know Your Brother, by Jackie Dodson with Jane Warnick

Know Your Elna, by Jackie Dodson with Carol Ahles

Know Your New Home, by Jackie Dodson with Judi Cull and Vicki Lynn Hastings

Know Your Pfaff, by Jackie Dodson with Audrey Griese

Know Your Sewing Machine, by Jackie Dodson

Know Your Simplicity, by Jackie Dodson with Jane Warnick

Know Your Singer, by Jackie Dodson

Know Your Viking, by Jackie Dodson with Jan Saunders

Know Your White, by Jackie Dodson with Jan Saunders

Owner's Guide to Sewing Machines, Sergers, and *Knitting Machines*, by Gale Grigg Hazen

Petite Pizzazz, by Barb Griffin

Sew, Serge, Press, by Jan Saunders

Sewing and Collecting Vintage Fashions, by Eileen MacIntosh

Other Books by the Authors, available from Chilton

Distinctive Serger Gifts and Crafts: An Idea Book for All Occasions

Special offer for *Simply Serge Any Fabric* readers: For a free sampler of articles and ideas from past issues of the *Serger Update* newsletter, send a business-sized, self-addressed, stamped envelope to: *Serger Update* Sampler Offer, 2269 Chestnut, Suite 269, Dept. SSF, San Francisco, CA 94123.

Refer to page 177 for other serger information written by the authors. In these books and publications, you'll find basic information on serging terms, stitch options, and sources for thread and general notions.

Simply Serge Any Fabric

A How-to Handbook for Today's Textiles

Naomi Baker and Tammy Young

Chilton Book Company
Radnor, Pennsylvania

Published in Radnor, Pennsylvania
19089 by Chilton Book Company

Color photographs by Lee Phillips
Designed by Martha Vercoutere
Cover design by Kevin Culver
Illustrations by Chris Hansen
Dressmaking by Naomi Baker

Manufactured in the United States of
America

Library of Congress Catalog Card
Number 89-83400

ISBN 0-8019-8104-2

2 3 4 5 6 7 8 9 0 9 8 7 6 5 4 3 2 1

Contents

Foreword

By Claire Shaeffer

While I was looking at computers recently, I overheard another customer talking about her serger. Naturally my ears perked up and I listened a little more closely. Imagine my disappointment when I realized that she was actually talking about her surge protector—not a serger.

In 1975 when I bought my first serger, very few homesewers had heard of a serger. I had a choice of two machines—not two brands, but two *machines*—from which to make my selection. Today there are dozens of serger models with features which will do almost anything, except cook dinner.

For me, a serger is like an umbrella: you don't need one every day, but when you do need one, nothing else will do. I am a very traditional homesewer; most of my sewing focuses on adapting ready-to-wear and couture techniques for the conventional sewing machine. So I don't think, much less use, my serger creatively. Fortunately, Tammy Young and Naomi Baker do; and they have created and tested a myriad of serging techniques for you and me.

In *Simply Serge Any Fabric*, Tammy and Naomi tell you everything you ever needed to know about serging fabrics. This practical book is filled with information for serging knits, wovens, fake fur fabrics, and man-made leathers, as well as offering some exciting patternless projects. And, in the unlikely event your serger has a bad day, the troubleshooting charts will help you understand its problems so you can cure its ills.

Oh, in case you're wondering, I'm not still serging on my original machine; I've advanced to a more sophisticated model.

Use this book as both a guide and an inspiration to serge on to greater projects!

Claire Shaeffer

Author,
Claire Shaeffer's Fabric Sewing Guide

Acknowledgments

Our sincere gratitude to all the serger-sewing enthusiasts who have helped and challenged us to write this book. Many of the techniques presented here were developed through the cooperative efforts of several people, all sharing ideas and inspiration.

First, a special thanks to Gail Brown, our friend, inspirational mentor, and Contributing Editor for the *Serger Update* newsletter (where we all work closely). Her fertile mind and vast reserves of sewing knowledge have helped us tremendously.

Thanks also to sewing pros Jan Saunders and Ann Beyer, who contributed research and background information to this book in the process of writing articles for the *Serger Update*.

The book could not have been completed without the diligent efforts of Lori Bottom, who is the Editorial Assistant for the *Serger Update* and who coordinated the manuscript. The other fully involved staff member is Chris Hansen, our talented illustrator, who also designs and sews beautifully. He's fine-tuned details in our illustration instructions more times than we care to admit.

Other *Update Newsletter* staff members have taken on an extra load to allow us to complete this book, and we give them a big thanks, too: Rad Dewey, Theresa Meintzer, Lisa Myers, Irene Lee, Jennifer Nguyen, and Leslie Wood.

Finally, a sincere thanks to our editor, Robbie Fanning, one of the best in the business. She's knowledgeable, highly organized, and a pleasure to work with.

The following are registered trademark names used in this book: *Antron III, Caress, Cordura, Facile, Gore-tex, Lamous II, Lycra, Pendleton, Seams Great, Scotch Magic Tape, Sofrina, Suedemark, Taslan, Tear-Away, ThreadFuse, Ultraleather, Ultrasuede,* and *Velcro.*

Introduction

When those of us in home-sewing first had access to sergers, those handy little overlock machines, serged seam finishes and seaming T-shirts and other casual sportswear were our most common projects. But as the art of serger sewing becomes more and more refined, many of us are having an even better time experimenting with "How can. . . ?" and "What if . . . ?" The results are special techniques and interesting decorative applications.

The *Serger Update* newsletter was started in response to this rapidly increasing demand for new serger tips, techniques, ideas, and inspiration. Now we use our sergers for projects we never considered before — inserting professional-looking zippers; creating a number of unique trims, including serger lace, binding, piping, and couching; and even speed-tailoring a blouse or jacket.

General Serging Guidelines

Serging most fabrics is a snap for anyone who has passed the beginning hurdles of serger use. Once you have mastered threading, tension adjustments, and stitch formation, general techniques usually apply.

Fabric weight is a major consideration in deciding how to seam, hem, and finish any project. **One important tip: Always** pretest on scraps of the actual fabric first.

Serging Special Fabrics

During the last year or two, our *Serger Update* staff has experimented with many hard-to-serge fabrics, ones for which general guidelines don't always apply. We've asked ourselves questions such as: "Can we serge real velvet?" "Are there any serger techniques to speed up sewing special-occasion fabrics?" "What about serging leather? Fur?"

Fabric-specific articles have been a big hit with our *Serger Update* subscribers. We've brainstormed, combined research from articles and booklets, done new testing, and compiled it all into this handy reference.

Each chapter outlines purchasing, pattern, and notion information for specialty fabrics. Handling tips, from layout and cutting to pressing and edge finishing, are also detailed. Special serging techniques for each fabric are given. In addition, easy patternless projects are included for specific fabrics. Use them to practice techniques, for lesson plans, or as quick gift ideas.

How to Use This Book

While there are several excellent serger books on the market with lots of good general technique information, this is the **first guide on serging all fabrics, including those that need special handling.** We hope you'll refer to it often as you continue to extend your serging possibilities.

Naomi Baker and Tammy Young

Guidelines – General Serging Options

	Seams	Seam Finishes	Edge Finishes	Hems
Lightweight	1. Narrow, medium-length, and balanced 3-thread stitch. 2. Rolled edge, short to medium length. 3. Narrow 3-thread flatlock. 4. Straight-stitch and serge seam allowances together.	1. Straight-stitch and serge seam allowances together. 2. Straight-stitch, serge seam allowances together, and press to one side. Secure with ThreadFuse or topstitching.	1. Rolled edge. 2. Narrow, medium-length and balanced 3-thread stitch.	1. Rolled edge. 2. Narrow, short- or medium-length and balanced 3-thread stitch. 3. Serge-finish, turn to wrong side, and edge-stitch. 4. Serge-finish, turn 5/8" to wrong side, edge-stitch, and topstitch.
Medium-weight	1. Wide, medium-length and balanced 3- or 3/4-thread stitch. 2. 3-thread flatlock, short to medium length. 3. Serge-finish, straight-stitch 5/8" seam, and press open. 4. Serge-finish, straight-stitch 5/8" seam, press open, and secure seam allowance with ThreadFuse or topstitching. 5. Straight-stitch and serge seam allowances together. 6. Straight-stitch, serge seam allowances together, and press to one side. Secure with Thread Fuse or topstitching.	1. Straight-stitch and serge seam allowances together. 2. Straight-stitch, serge seam allowances together, and press to one side. Secure with ThreadFuse or topstitching. 3. Straight-stitch, serge seam allowances together, press to one side, and edge- and topstitch (see Chapter 7, pages 116-117).	1. Self-binding (see Chapter 7, page 118). 2. Faux-braid (see Chapter 7, pages 118-119, and Chapter 9, pages 147-148).	1. Serge-finish, turn to wrong side, and edge-stitch. 2. Serge-finish, turn 5/8" to wrong side, edge-stitch, and topstitch. 3. Serge-finish. Turn to wrong side and hand-stitch, machine blind-stitch, or topstitch.
Heavy-weight	1. Serge-finish, straight-stitch 5/8" seam, and press open. 2. Wide 3-thread flatlock. 3. Serge-finish, lap, and edge-stitch. 4. Serge-finish, straight-stitch 5/8" seam, topstitch, and edge-stitch.	1. Serge-finish.	1. Faux-braid (see Chapter 7, pages 118-119, and Chapter 9, pages 147-148). 2. Reversible-edge binding (see Chapter 11, page 162). 3. Self-binding (see Chapter 7, page 118).	1. Serge-finish, turn to wrong side, and hand-stitch or machine blind-stitch. 2. Serge-finish, turn to wrong side, and topstitch.

Notions Guidelines for Specialty Fabrics

Selecting appropriate notions for your specialty fabric projects can make the difference between "I'll never be able to serge this fabric!" and "This wasn't so difficult after all!". Often personal preference will dictate your choice of notions. Specific fabrics within a general category may also need special handling, so when in doubt, be sure to test first.

Timesaving Notions

Fabric	Scissors and Cutters	Needles*	Pins	Seaming Thread	Special Threads	Marking
Interlocks and Jerseys	sharp scissors no rotary cutter	fine, sharp 9/65, 10/70, or 11/75	long, fine	all-purpose serger	woolly stretch nylon ThreadFuse	air-erasable or water-soluble markers, no tracing wheel
Sweaterknits	sharp scissors no rotary cutter	sharp or ballpoint 14/90	long, large heads	all-purpose, serger, woolly stretch nylon	woolly stretch nylon	cut out notches, no markers
Stretch Fabrics	sharp scissors rotary cutter and mat	fine, sharp 9/65, 10/70 or 11/75 — universal or ballpoint	long	all-purpose, serger, woolly stretch nylon	woolly stretch nylon ThreadFuse	air-erasable or water-soluble markers, notch narrow seam allowances (don't clip)
Lingerie Fabrics	sharp scissors rotary cutter and mat	fine, sharp 9/65, 10/70, or 11/75	long, fine	lingerie, serger, woolly stretch nylon	ThreadFuse, rayon woolly stretch nylon	air-erasable or water-soluble markers
Silk and Silky Fabrics	sharp scissors serrated scissors rotary cutter	fine, sharp 9/65, 10/70, or 11/75	long, fine	lingerie serger	ThreadFuse, rayon woolly stretch nylon	no marking pens for silks, no water-soluble markers for dry-clean-only fabrics, test markers on other silky fabrics
Special-Occasion Fabrics	sharp scissors no rotary cutter	fine, sharp 9/65, 10/70, or 11/75 ballpoint for metallics	long, fine masking tape	lingerie serger	monofilament nylon for topstitching lace, metallic, woolly stretch nylon	test air-erasable no water-soluble
Denim, Canvas, and Tapestry	sharp scissors rotary cutter and mat	sharp 11/80 to 16/100, depending on fabric weight	long	all-purpose serger	ThreadFuse, pearl rayon buttonhole twist, pearl cotton woolly stretch nylon	no water-soluble on tapestry
Pile Fabrics	sharp scissors serrated scissors rotary cutter and mat	sharp 11/75 to 14/90, depending on fabric weight	long, large heads	all-purpose serger	ThreadFuse woolly stretch nylon buttonhole twist	no water-soluble on velvet
Suedes, Leathers, and Synthetics	sharp scissors rotary cutter and mat	sharp 11/80 to 14/90, depending on fabric weight	long	all-purpose serger	ThreadFuse, pearl rayon buttonhole twist, pearl cotton woolly stretch nylon	test marking pens
Fake Furs	sharp scissors, single-edge razor blade rotary cutter and mat	sharp 14/90 to 16/100, depending on fabric weight	none with leather and suede	all-purpose serger	woolly stretch nylon	test marking pens
Quilted Fabrics and Vinyls	sharp rotary cutter and mat	fine, sharp 11/80 or smaller	none	lingerie serger	none	air-erasable or water-soluble markers

*Always start each project with a new needle.

Pattern weights—Useful for holding the pattern and fabric in place while cutting, weights eliminate the need for pinning. Pattern weights are good for bulky fabrics that are difficult to pin and essential for fabrics that should not be pinned.

Seaming thread—The most common seaming threads are all-purpose sewing thread and serger thread. Polyester or cotton-wrapped polyester all-purpose thread is readily available. Serger thread is also polyester or cotton-wrapped polyester but is lighter in weight and often comes in larger yardages. Polyester is resilient and will stretch with the fabric. Lingerie thread is even lighter weight and a good choice for lingerie, silky, special-occasion, or vinyl fabrics. Woolly stretch nylon (see below) and #80 nylon monofilament are also possible seaming choices. When in doubt as to the best thread to use for seams, test on a scrap of actual garment fabric.

Special threads—Decorative threads play a large part in the excitement of serger sewing. Possibilities abound, but testing is essential. Woolly stretch nylon, metallic thread, buttonhole twist, #8 pearl cotton, and rayon thread are old favorites. A new possibility is pearl rayon.

Woolly stretch nylon—One of our favorite decorative threads for serger sewing. A crimped nylon thread, it is soft and stretchy and fluffs out to fill between stitches. Use this thread in needle(s) and loopers for a balanced tension stitch, or use only in the upper looper for a rolled edge. You may need to loosen the tensions to allow the thread to fluff up after serging.

Rayon thread—A bright-colored, inexpensive, silk-like thread. It is weaker than silk, so use it only in the upper looper for decorative stitching. You may have to increase the tension for the stitch to lie smoothly. For a balanced stitch, use rayon thread in both loopers and serger thread in the needle. For serging a rolled edge, use rayon thread in the upper looper, serger thread in the needle, and #80 nylon monofilament or woolly stretch nylon in the lower looper.

Metallic thread—Use this thread only in the loopers. For rolled edges, combine it with fine nylon monofilament thread (#80) in the needle and lower looper. When using metallic thread, you may have to loosen the looper tension(s). Combine fine metallic thread with woolly stretch nylon (both in the upper looper) for better strength and edge coverage. When using double strands, loosen the tension for uniform feeding.

ThreadFuse—A combination of polyester thread twisted with fusible fibers. When fused, the thread remains intact. The fusible bond is soft and pliable but very strong. It is not affected by laundering or dry cleaning. Use *ThreadFuse* in the lower looper or in the bobbin of your sewing machine with a medium to wide stitch width to provide maximum coverage. Tighten the lower looper tension slightly to pull the *ThreadFuse* to the wrong side.

Marking pens—Air-erasable and/or water-soluble marking pens are very useful on some fabrics but are not appropriate for others. Before using on any fabric, always test on scraps of fabric to ensure best results.

Knits

1. Interlock and Jersey Techniques

Knits are plentiful in everyone's wardrobe, from knock-around T's to dinner dresses. The easy fit of knit, plus its wrinkle resistance and ease of sewing, makes it the sewing choice for beginners to most-experienced seamsters. Emulate the best of jersey and interlock ready-to-wear by simply serging with fast, easy techniques to produce professional-looking knit fashions.

Fabric Choices

To say that knits have changed is an understatement. Early problems included unbreathable polyester knits and a limited selection of other knits that didn't hold their shape; but today we have myriad knit options available (Fig. 1-1).

• INTERLOCKS (FINE RIB) • JERSEYS (SINGLE KNIT)

Fig. 1-1

Interlocks

Interlocks are enjoying unprecedented popularity—and for good reason. These stretchy, drapeable knits are actually a fine double rib. The rib pattern is nearly indiscernible, but you'll recognize interlocks by their beefy hand and crosswise stretchability. Interlocks hold their shape well and are more stable than jerseys. An interlock is suitable as its own edge finish, can be reversed for use on either side, and is available in many fiber types. It has **up to 50% stretch,** and has **good recovery.**

Singleknit Jerseys

This fabric comes in an incredible range of weights, textures, and fibers. Most common are fine T-shirt weights, but this category includes much heavier sweatshirting, brushed on the wrong side for comfort and body.

Jerseys have a definite right and wrong side. They appear flat and smooth on the right side and have crosswise rows of loops on the wrong side. **When stretched crosswise, the edge will curl to the right side of the fabric and, when pulled lengthwise, the edge will curl to the wrong side of the fabric.**

Jerseys may have a permanent crease lengthwise, down the center of the fabric. They are softer and less stable than interlocks, and the jersey rib may run in the lengthwise direction. They have **up to 50% stretch,** and their **recovery is fair.**

The addition of *Lycra* **(spandex) fiber to a jersey gives two-way stretch to the fabric.** *Lycra* was once related to swim- and aerobicwear only; now it is being sewn into dresses and separates.

Jersey with *Lycra* **has several performance bonuses,** including minimal bagging and wrinkling. **It usually has 100%-plus stretch in both the lengthwise and crosswise directions and full recovery.**

Pattern Selection

Because knit fabric is made of interlocking loops, almost every knit has some built-in stretch. **Select a pattern designed for knit fabric** and follow the fabric recommendations for the pattern. Jerseys are categorized as lightweight knits and interlocks as medium-weight knits.

Because the stretch of the fabric will affect how the garment fits, **it is important to follow the stretch ratio or gauge provided with the pattern.**

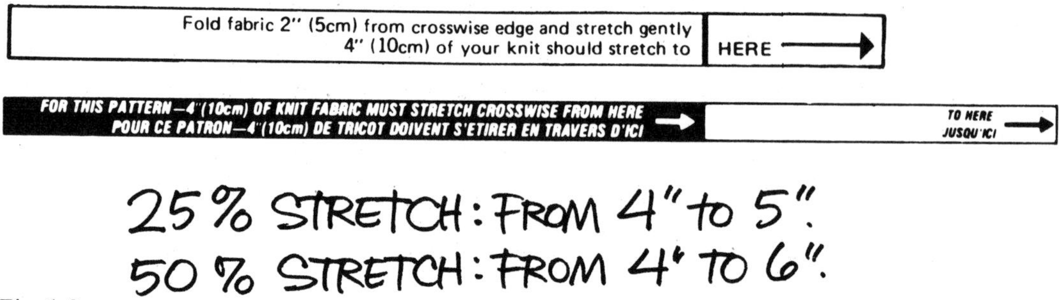

25% STRETCH: FROM 4" to 5".
50% STRETCH: FROM 4" to 6".

Fig. 1-2

To determine the stretch ratio of your fabric, simply fold 2" in the crosswise direction, then stretch 4" along the fold in the true crosswise direction. If it stretches 1/2", the ratio is about 12.5%, 2" is 50%, and so on (Fig. 1-2). Some patterns specify two different ratios for the same style; 50% or more stretch may be needed for the ribbed bands, but only 25% may be required for the main body of the garment.

Why is it crucial to follow stretch guidelines? Because the stretch allows the pattern designer to exclude fitting features like darts and wearing ease; the knit shapes to and moves with the body without darted-in contours or extra ease. Also, stretch and recovery minimize inner construction and fasteners; facingless edges can be turned and topstitched (even on curves), and garments can be pulled on without zippered openings.

If you choose a knit that doesn't stretch to pattern specifications, your finished garment may be too tight, distorted, or, worse yet, impossible to pull on over your head or hips.

Recovery is the degree of resilience, or the amount the knit springs back into shape. Give any prospective knit a test stretch, not only for pattern compatibility, but to forecast its performance under wearing conditions. Does it spring back or remain stretched out? Forget fabrics that don't recover.

Fitting Knits

This is not an exact science, but it is an easily acquired aptitude because the fabric is so forgiving.

• **The stretchier the knit, the tighter the fit can be.**

• **Compensate** for knits with 50% or more stretch and marginal recovery (like 100% cotton interlocks and sweaterings) **by sizing down a pattern size.** Cut out your standard size and, after a fitting check, sew wider (1") seam allowances.

• **If working with a knit that stretches less than the pattern suggests,** offset the difference by cutting the pattern larger—try an extra 1/2" along all major seamlines. Pin-fit before the final seaming.

Timesaving Notions

✎ **Note:** For more notions information, refer to the general Timesaving

Notions section in the Introduction and the Notions Guidelines for Specialty Fabrics chart on page *x*. Notions with fabric-specific explanations are explained here.

- **Scissors**

- **Pattern weights**

- **Machine needles**—A dull or damaged needle will cut the knit or make holes on the seamline. Adjust the needle size for light- or medium-weight fabric.

- **Pins**

- **All-purpose thread or serger thread**

- **Woolly stretch nylon**

- *ThreadFuse*

- **Marking pen**

Interfacing

Often jerseys and interlocks need no interfacing, especially if interfacing might interfere with the drape of the fabric. If the garment requires stabilization in collars, cuffs, or facings, **interface with a lightweight fusible interfacing.** Use one that moves and drapes with the knit. Select a fusible knit tricot for soft stabilization and a fusible, bias, nonwoven interfacing for more crispness.

Pretreat fusible interfacing by steam-shrinking it after cutting, just prior to fusing.

1. Press the fashion-fabric where the interfacing will be applied. Then position the interfacing, resin side down.

2. Hold the steam iron an inch above the interfacing and steam generously for a few seconds. Use the burst-of-steam feature on your iron, if you have it. You can often see the edges of the interfacing draw up slightly as you steam; the slight change in size due to shrinking does not affect the finished product. See Fig. 1-3.

INTERFACE WITH FUSIBLES

Fig. 1-3

It's usually safer to **fuse interfacing to the facing rather than to the garment** (Fig. 1-3); to decrease bulk, trim off about 1/2" from the interfacing seam allowances before fusing. Test swatches on fabric scraps to assess suitability.

Fabric Preparation

Knits should be pretreated to allow for shrinkage, remove sizing, and relax the fabric after having been wound on bolts.

- **Prelaunder washable knits.** Some 100%-cotton interlocks will shrink as much as 8" in length per yard (nearly 25%!). **Machine wash and dry *twice*.**

- **Dry-clean-only knits should be thoroughly steamed or bulk-cleaned by a dry cleaner.** With hefty steam treatment, shrinkage can be as much as 4" in length per yard.

Pattern Layout and Cutting

• **Watch for permanent fold lines.** Refold, if necessary, so that the line will be cut away. Or, if the layout is tight, position the line in an inconspicuous area, such as the center of the sleeves.

• **Follow "with nap" layouts,** if possible, because of one-way, directional knit construction.

• If using a run-prone synthetic interlock, effectively prevent running by cutting out garment pieces so that the fabric runs up from the hems (which are subjected to less stress).

• To secure pattern pieces, **use weights** or fine, sharp, long pins with large heads.

• **If the fabric is tubular, cut it apart on the crease before laying it out.**

• For better accuracy, **cut striped fabric in a single layer.**

• **Do not let fabric hang over the cutting surface edge** because knit fabric will stretch out of shape.

• **Check for the right side of jersey fabric by pulling across the grain;** the horizontal cut edge will curl to the right side (Fig. 1-4).

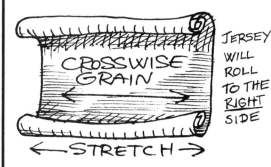

Fig. 1-4

Pressing

Press jerseys and interlocks with a steam iron in an up-and-down motion in the lengthwise direction. Pressing across the grain will distort the knit and may permanently stretch it out of shape. Allow the fabric to dry completely before handling.

Do not overpress wool jersey. Use a dry iron and a slightly dampened press cloth (Fig. 1-5). Stop pressing while the fabric is still steaming and damp. Because wool absorbs moisture, allow extra time for the fabric to cool before moving it.

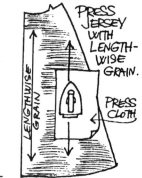

Fig. 1-5

Wool jersey is easily molded and eased by steam pressing, a definite advantage for necklines, sleeve caps, and hems.

Seams and Seam Finishes

To prevent stretched-out, wavy seams in knits, try one of the following tips:

• **Adjust the differential feed to a 2.0 ratio setting** to automatically ease the fabric.

• **Ease-plus as you serge** (Fig. 1-6). With one index finger, hold the fabric behind the presser foot. With the other hand, force-feed the fabric under the foot faster than the feed dogs take it in. The resulting seam will be slightly eased.

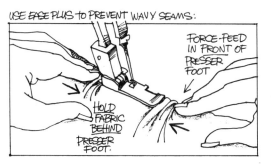

Fig. 1-6

• **Lessen the pressure on the presser foot.**

The flattest, least conspicuous seam for interlocks is a 5/8" seam pressed open. On jerseys, traditional pressed-open seams seldom stay that way because the fabric will curl.

• For interlocks, **serge-finish the garment edges and straight-stitch the 5/8" seam allowances.** Press open and topstitch from the right side (Fig. 1-7).

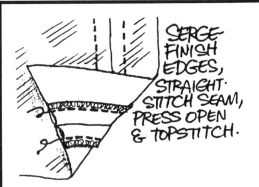

Fig. 1-7

• **For jerseys or interlocks, straight-stitch 5/8" seam allowances, serge together, and topstitch to one side** (Fig. 1-8).

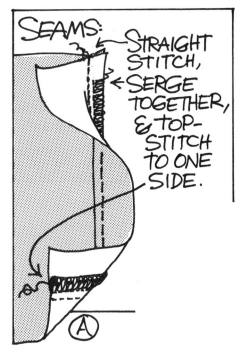

Fig. 1-8

The inherent stretch of a serged stitch makes it perfect for seaming knits. No stretching is necessary as you serge. **A 3- or 3/4-thread stitch has**

built-in stretch and both can be used for seaming (Fig. 1-9).

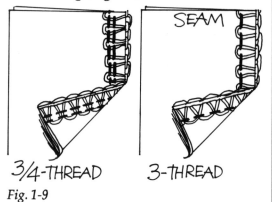

Fig. 1-9

1. **Adjust the serger for a long** (3.5 to 4mm), **wide, and balanced stitch.** The longer stitch length will help prevent wavy seams.

2. With right sides together, serge-seam the garment. Press the seam to one side and topstitch to secure. **For variation, use** *ThreadFuse* **in the lower looper when seaming.** Carefully press the seam to one side and fuse to secure.

Decorative Seams

Decorative serging is easily done on knit fabric, from the right side (Fig. 1-10). To avoid overdoing the decorative look, serge the side seams right sides together.

Flatlocking combines seaming and topstitching in one step, giving a neat bulk-free finish. Flatlocking works best with interlock knit fabric. Follow these simple steps:

1. **Thread the serger with decorative or contrasting thread in the upper looper.**

Fig. 1-10

2. **Adjust the serger for 3-thread flatlocking by loosening the needle tension and tightening the lower looper tension.** The needle thread should be loose enough to overlock with the upper looper thread beyond the edge of the fabric (Fig. 1-11). Adjust the serger for a wide width and a short length.

3. Place the wrong sides of the fabric together and **serge the edge,** allowing

3-THREAD FLATLOCK:

NEEDLE THREAD LOOSENED TO INTERLOCK WITH UPPER LOOPER THREAD BEYOND EDGE. LOWER LOOPER TIGHTENED TO A STRAIGHT LINE.

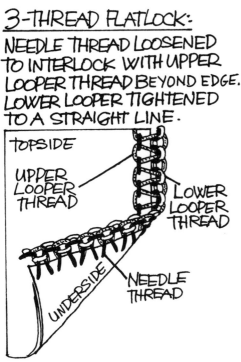

TOPSIDE

UPPER LOOPER THREAD

LOWER LOOPER THREAD

UNDERSIDE

NEEDLE THREAD

Fig. 1-11

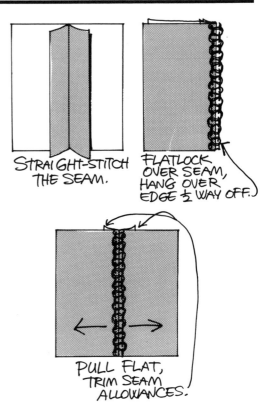

STRAIGHT-STITCH THE SEAM.

FLATLOCK OVER SEAM, HANG OVER EDGE ½ WAY OFF.

PULL FLAT, TRIM SEAM ALLOWANCES.

Fig. 1-12

the stitches to hang over the edge of the fabric.

4. Pull the seam apart until it lies flat.

For a more durable flatlocked seam:

1. **Straight-stitch the seam using standard 5/8" seam allowances** (adding durability and finishing the seamline). For most knits, a longer stitch length (about 8-9/inch) produces the smoothest seam. Press open.

2. Fold the seam wrong sides together. Align the seamline on the fold. Using the widest stitch width, **flatlock over the folded seam.** To facilitate the **flattest flatlocking and centering of the stitches,** allow them to hang over the folded edge about half the stitch width, as shown (Fig. 1-12).

3. Pull the seam flat. Press lightly if necessary. Trim the allowances to the stitching.

A **faux-flatlocked seam is done with a balanced stitch** and is more durable than flatlocking:

1. Adjust the serger for a wide, short, and balanced 3- or 3/4-thread stitch. Use decorative or contrasting thread in the upper looper and all-purpose or serger thread in the needle and lower looper.

2. Serge the seam wrong sides together.

3. Press the seam to one side and edge-stitch.

For variation, use *ThreadFuse* in the lower looper and fuse the serged seam to secure, eliminating the edge stitching.

Stabilizing Seams

Stabilization is usually unnecessary for most seams. But for shoulder seams on stretchy fabrics, serge the seams, press toward the garment back, and topstitch (Fig. 1-13). For soft stabilization of a waistline seam, place a bias tricot strip, such as *Seams Great,* on the seamline, then sew over it.

STABILIZING WOOL JERSEY:

STABILIZE SHOULDER SEAMS BY PRESSING SEAM ALLOWANCES TOWARD BACK & TOP-STITCHING.

STABILIZE WAIST SEAM BY SEWING OVER SEAMS GREAT CENTERED ON 5/8" SEAM.

Fig. 1-13

Edge Finishing

On knits with 25% stretch, finish the edges easily by turning and top-stitching the seam allowances (Fig. 1-14). Test on garment scraps first to see if this method provides enough stability and allows the edge to turn smoothly. Also be sure the neckline edge fits over your head. Here's how:

1. **Serge-finish the edge and turn the allowance 3/8" to 1/2" to the wrong side;** pin intermittently.

2. **Topstitch 1/4" to 3/8" from the fold,** using a single or twin needle, stretching as you sew.

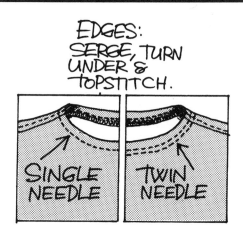

EDGES: SERGE, TURN UNDER & TOPSTITCH.

SINGLE NEEDLE   TWIN NEEDLE

Fig. 1-14

Variation I: For reversible interlocks, serge-finish, turn to the right side, and edge-stitch through the serging loops (Fig. 1-15).

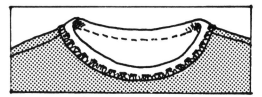

OR SERGE, TURN TO RIGHT SIDE, & EDGESTITCH.

Fig. 1-15

Variation II: Serge-finish with *ThreadFuse* in the lower looper. Press carefully to the right or wrong side and fuse to secure. Edge-stitch if needed.

Self Binding

For a beefier, more-stable edge finish, serge a self-binding. Because the wrong side shows, self-binding is best for knits with similar right and wrong sides. Also, maneuvering the serger foot is easiest around a more open, gradually curved neckline.

1. **Cut the neckline edge with a 7/8" allowance.**

2. Thread the needle and loopers with serger or all-purpose thread. **Adjust for a 5mm-wide, medium-length and balanced 3-thread stitch.**

3. **Serge the shoulder seams wrong sides together. Topstitch the serged seam** toward the back of the shoulder seam.

4. Serge-finish the neckline edge from the wrong side.

5. Fold the serged neck edge 7/8" to the wrong side and serge along the fold, as shown (Fig. 1-16).

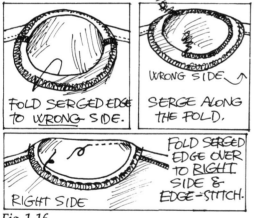

Fig. 1-16

6. Wrap the serged edge over to the right side and edge-stitch in place.

Binding the Edge

Bind the neck or armhole with ribbing-by-the-yard or self-fabric. An advantage of this binding is that the neckline or edge will never stretch out. The finished binding should not be wider than 1". Here's how:

1. Cut crosswise strips three times the finished binding width plus 1/2". The length will be the edge measurement plus 1". Serge-finish one long edge.

2. Serge one shoulder seam.

3. Right sides together, straight-stitch the binding to the edge (Fig. 1-17).

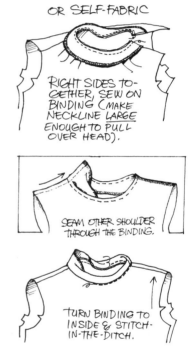

Fig. 1-17

Seam allowances should be the width of the finished trim. Stretch slightly around curves so that the finished binding will lie flat. **Caution:** After pinning the other shoulder seam, pull the bound edge over your head (it should be large enough to pull on and off easily).

4. Straight-stitch the other shoulder seam, through the binding, and press open. Trim the seam bulk.

5. Fold the binding over the seam and stitch-in-the-ditch to secure it in place (Fig. 1-17).

✎ **Note:** Follow this same procedure for binding the armhole edges.

Self-Fabric Bands

Finish the neck or armhole with self-fabric bands. Use this method when light- to medium-weight knits call for a stable but soft edge finish. The flat construction method allows for taking in or letting out the last band seam—helpful when making fit adjustments.

1. Cut the self-fabric-band length along either the crosswise or the greatest stretch direction. Cut the band 2" wide by the edge measurement plus 1".

2. Serge one shoulder seam.

3. Fold the band in half lengthwise, wrong sides together (Fig. 1-18). Then serge the band to the right side of the neck edge.

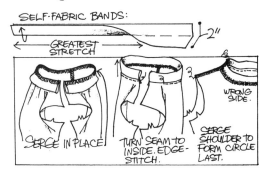

Fig. 1-18

4. Turn the seam allowance to the inside. From the right side, edge-stitch through all layers 1/8" on the garment side of the seamline.

5. Serge the other shoulder seam and binding (forming a circle). Hide any seam allowances that show on the finished edge by hand tacking them to the wrong side.

✎ **Note:** Follow the same procedure for finishing the armhole edges.

Fast Hems

Before hemming, **allow the garment to hang for 24 hours.**

A serger finishes the hem of a knit garment quickly and easily. Here are some options:

• **Simply serge-finish with narrow rolled or balanced hemming.** Lengthen the stitch for a lighter, less decorative hem. This hem is a fast, swingy finish for flared jersey skirts and dresses. Also, finish in this manner before pleating knits—there's no bulk to interfere with pressing.

☞ **Special Tip:** Flounce (lettuce leaf) edges and hems easily (Fig. 1-19). Stretch while satin-serging. The more stretch, the more flounce. If possible, flounce before seaming in a circle to keep the hem edge flat for easier, more even stretching.

• **Serge, turn up 1/2" to the wrong side, and topstitch 1/4" from the hemline** (Fig. 1-20). **Optional:** Topstitch with a double or triple needle. This technique is recommended for most knits.

• For a wider hem, **serge, turn up to the wrong side, and double- or triple-**

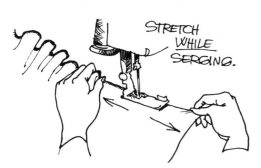

Fig. 1-19

• SERGE-FINISH WITH NARROW ROLLED OR BALANCED HEMMING.

• SERGE, TURN UP ½" & TOPSTITCH

• SERGE, TURN UP & DOUBLE-NEEDLE TOPSTITCH.

Fig. 1-20

needle topstitch 1/2" to 2" from the hemline.

• Serge-finish the edge with *Thread-Fuse* in the lower looper. Turn the hem allowance to the wrong side and fuse carefully. No topstitching is necessary.

• **Blindstitched hem:** Serge-finish, then turn up, fold, and blindstitch as shown (Fig. 1-21). For a discreetly stitched hem, the zigzag portion of the blind-stitch should barely catch the fold. Adjust the stitch length and width to achieve the most inconspicuous hem. Always test on scraps.

SERGE-FINISH, THEN BLINDSTITCH BY MACHINE.

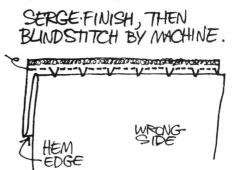

WRONG SIDE

HEM EDGE

Fig. 1-21

• **Make serged, machine-stitched pant hems completely invisible** (Fig. 1-22).

INVISIBLE MACHINE-STITCHED PANT

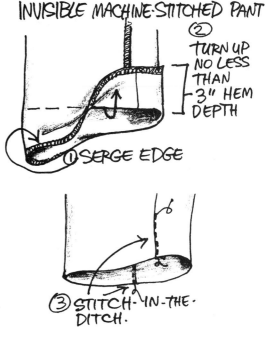

② TURN UP NO LESS THAN 3" HEM DEPTH

① SERGE EDGE

③ STITCH-IN-THE-DITCH.

Fig. 1-22

Allow no less than a 3" hem depth. Serge-finish the raw edges of the pantlegs. Then simply turn up, aligning the out-seams and the in-seams, and stitch-in-the-ditch from the right side. This method is super-quick and truly invisible, but care must be taken when stepping into the pantleg. Perfect for straight- and tapered-leg pants made of any weight knit.

• **Use a faux-flatlocked hem** for a decorative hem finish. Serge-finish the hem edge, press to the right side, and topstitch (Fig. 1-23). If the fabric has a definite right and wrong side, forget this technique—just press up the hem to the wrong side and topstitch.

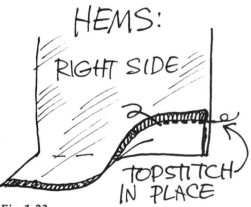

Fig. 1-23

Special Techniques

Serge-Setting Creases

Knits resist permanent creasing. **Creases can be set in pants or pleated skirts** with the serger. There are two methods for serge-setting creases (Fig. 1-24). For both, use a 3-thread stitch and all-purpose or serger thread throughout. Test on same-grain garment fabric scraps until you achieve the look you want.

Fig. 1-24

Narrow Rolled-Edge Creasing
(Fig. 1-25):

1. Press the garment along the creaseline.

2. Adjust for medium-length (2 to 3mm), narrow rolled-edge hemming.

3. Serge along the fold, being careful not to cut the fold.

☞ **Special Tip:** If you have a blind-hem foot, use it to ensure cut-free serging along the fold.

Flatlocked Creasing
(Fig. 1-25):

1. Press-mark the garment along the creaseline.

2. Adjust for narrow, medium-length flatlocking. Do not loosen the needle thread completely; a slightly tightened needle thread will cause the flatlocking to form a crease.

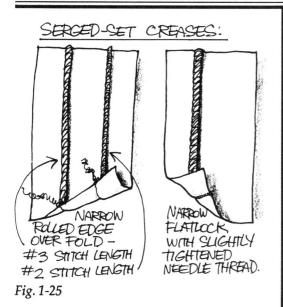

SERGED-SET CREASES:

NARROW ROLLED EDGE OVER FOLD – #3 STITCH LENGTH #2 STITCH LENGTH

NARROW FLATLOCK WITH SLIGHTLY TIGHTENED NEEDLE THREAD.

Fig. 1-25

✎ **Note:** For the skirt shown (Fig. 1-24), alternate the fold directions and serge on alternating sides of the fabric. If the first serge-set crease shows on the right side, serge the next crease on the wrong side. Alternating the crease direction will simulate the look of pleats.

Facings

Facings are easily finished using the serger (Fig. 1-26). **Interface, then finish the facing edge with serging—a**

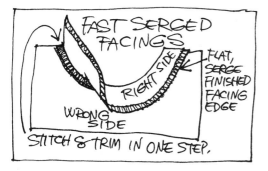

FAST SERGED FACINGS

RIGHT SIDE

WRONG SIDE

FLAT, SERGE FINISHED FACING EDGE

STITCH & TRIM IN ONE STEP.

Fig. 1-26

change from bulky, time-consuming clean finishing.

Place the facing right sides together on the edge and serge the seam. The result is a flat, smooth, more durable seam that requires no trimming or clipping.

Buttonholes

Most knit garments are made without closures, but you may want buttonholes for some garments (Fig. 1-27). Here are some tips:

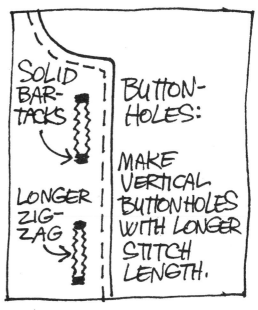

SOLID BAR-TACKS

LONGER ZIG-ZAG

BUTTON-HOLES:

MAKE VERTICAL BUTTONHOLES WITH LONGER STITCH LENGTH.

Fig. 1-27

• **Sew buttonholes in the lengthwise direction of the fabric** for less stretching of the garment.

• **Stabilize buttonholes with a layer of tear-away interfacing** under the fabric while stitching.

• **Use a longer-than-usual stitch length** to avoid stretching.

Easiest Serging Order

Follow the fastest flat-construction serging order (Fig. 1-28). Finish hemming the neckline, sleeves, and lower edge after serging the seams.

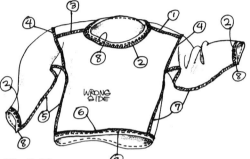

Fig. 1-28

1. Serge one shoulder seam.

2. Serge-finish the neckline and lower sleeves.

3. Serge the other shoulder seam.

4. Serge the sleeves to the garment.

5. Serge one side seam from the lower edge through the underarm to the sleeve seam.

6. Serge-finish the lower edge.

7. Serge the other side, underarm and sleeve seam.

8. Topstitch hems on neckline, sleeves, and the lower edge.

Quick Tips

• When choosing a fabric for a pattern, check ready-to-wear. **If a popular design is shown in a particular fabric, it will also be suitable for your pattern.**

• **Eliminate a back zipper from a garment if the knit fabric has a lot of** stretch and will fit over your head. Also eliminate the seam by cutting the back of the garment on the fold.

• Most knit sleeves don't need easing to be sewn into the armhole. Matching the notches, **serge sleeves with the bodice on top,** allowing the feed dogs to do the necessary easing.

• To stabilize fabric when applying a zipper, **fuse a strip of lightweight interfacing to the seam allowance** before sewing the zipper.

• **When topstitching with a single needle, stretch while stitching** to prevent popped stitches. Steam the hem after stitching.

Project: Quick-Serged Robe
(Fig. 1-29)

Fig. 1-29

This robe fits Sizes 36 to 38, bust or chest. To enlarge the pattern, add width to the side seams at the front, back, and sleeve. Adjust the length at the lower edges.

Serger Settings

Allow 1/4" seam allowances. Adjust the serger for a **wide, balanced stitch.** Use a medium length for serge-seaming and a shorter length for serge-finishing. If desired, use a decorative or contrasting thread for serge-finishing.

Cutting Directions

The robe is cut from **2 yards of 60"-wide interlock.** Cut robe pieces from the measurements shown (Fig. 1-30).

(Refer to Fig. 1-31 for Steps 1 through 9.)

1. With right sides together, **serge-seam both shoulder seams and the short ends of the belt.**

2. Adjust the serger for serge-finishing. From the wrong side, **serge-finish the upper edge of the pocket, the edges of the neckline and front, and the lower edges of the sleeves.**

3. Press a 2" hem to the right side of the pocket and topstitch. **Serge-finish the side and lower edge of the pocket.**

4. **Topstitch the pocket to the right front of the robe on the placement lines,** as shown (Fig. 1-30).

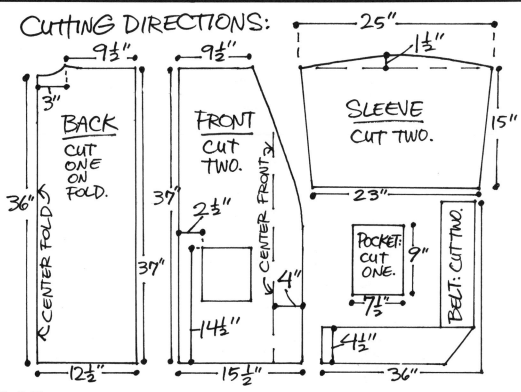

Fig. 1-30

5. Fold the belt in half lengthwise, wrong sides together, and **serge-finish the cut edges.**

6. Adjust the serger for serge-seaming. Matching the center of the sleeve to the shoulder seam, **serge-seam the sleeves to the garment. Serge-seam the side and underarm seams.**

7. **Serge-finish the lower edge.**

8. **Turn 1/2" to the right side** on the lower sleeve edges, neckline, and front edges. **Topstitch.**

9. **Turn 1" to the wrong side at the lower edge and topstitch.**

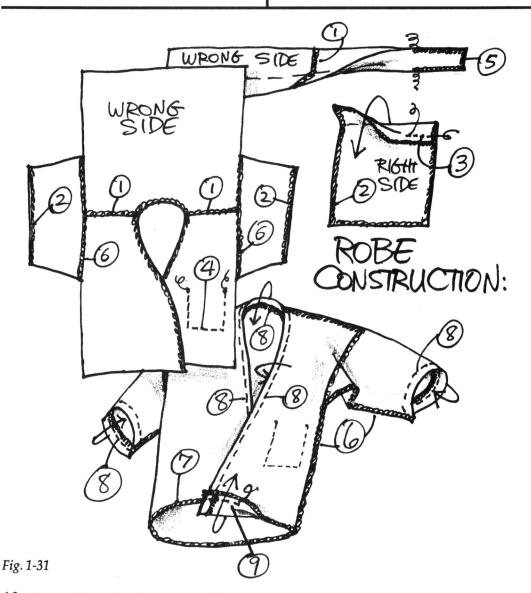

Fig. 1-31

2. Sweaterknit Secrets

Sweaters are easier to sew than ever before. Sweaterknits and ribbing are readily available to the home sewer. Fitting and sewing can be done easily even by a novice seamstress. For little money, an expensive boutique sweater can be copied in an hour or two. Sweaters can be serged quickly and simply with professional results.

Fabric Choices

Select the most suitable, sewable sweatering and your job's nearly done. Knit fabric variations are vast, but most sweaterknits are single knits. Plain jerseys look like hand-knitted stockinette stitches on the right side and purl stitches on the wrong side, whereas rib knits are alternating jersey and purl stitches. Another popular category for home-sewers is raschel knits. With these knits, lengthwise rows of interlocking loops stabilize the other yarns in a loose or lacy construction.

The key to selecting the right fabric is to test before buying. Stretch a small section of the knit to determine its resiliency (the amount it stretches back). If the knit doesn't have adequate recovery, chances are your well-intentioned sewing efforts will be wasted on a sweater that will stretch at the neckline, elbows, and cuffs. In general, stretch and recovery are most crucial in the crosswise grain direction, so the sweatering shapes, but doesn't sag, over body contours. Obviously resiliency is essential for ribbing and ribbed trims, because both are used to control stretch at garment edges. Don't forget to consider fiber characteristics and care.

✎ **Note:** Blends of two or more fibers, usually a synthetic and a natural fiber, often bring out the best properties of both.

Acrylic

Acrylic is the most common fiber found in sweaterings. To minimize stretching and pilling, buy the best quality you can afford. **Tightly constructed acrylic knits have excellent resiliency.** Machine wash and tumble dry (remove promptly) to avoid wrinkles, pilling, and long-term limpness.

Cotton
(Fig. 2-1):

Although one of the most durable and comfortable fibers, cotton is probably the most mishandled ready-to-sew sweaterknit. **Resiliency is fair to poor.** Enhance it by prewashing and drying to compact the fibers, decrease stretching out, and ensure easy machine care of the garment. Cottons are quite resistant to pilling but are shrink-prone, so prewash and dry twice.

COMMON COTTON SWEATERING

JERSEY KNIT (RIGHT SIDE)   (WRONG SIDE)

RIBBING (RIGHT OR WRONG SIDE.)

Fig. 2-1

For more stability and body, use ribbing-by-the-yard for the entire sweater; finer, 1 knit by 1 purl ribbing (2 knit by 2 purl is illustrated, Fig. 2-1) is less bulky and can easily double as sweater fabric.

Wool

Probably the easiest sweatering to sew and serge, wool is also the most expensive and hard to find. Also, wool must be dry cleaned or carefully hand-washed. It has **unbeatable resiliency;** use a steam iron for blocking and shaping.

Rayon

Rayon is seen most frequently as a shiny slub in a blend rather than as the sole fiber in a sweaterknit. It has **fair to poor resiliency** and is weak when wet. However, most of these short-comings are mitigated when rayon is blended with more resilient and/or stronger fibers (like wool or cotton) in a tightly constructed knit. Pure rayon sweaterings are irresistibly slinky but demand special sewing techniques and care. Rayon sweater making is not for beginners.

Metallics

Usually blended with other fibers for decorative effects, **metallics have poor resiliency** (usually not a problem when integrated sparingly throughout the knit design). If washability is important, check care instructions (the more metallic yarn, the greater likelihood of dry-clean-only status).

Sweatering Options

Yardage

Sweatering is readily available by the yard at most fabric stores. The width is about 54" to 60" and yardage is the most stable of the sweaterings included here. It's the recommended choice for a novice. To avoid possible unavailability later, buy matching trim, coordinating ribbed bands, or ribbed yardage when you buy sweater yardage.

Sweater Bodies

Sold individually or in a kit, a sweater body is a finished length of knit with a knit-in ribbed band (Fig. 2-2). Additional finishing of hem

Fig. 2-2

edges is unnecessary. **Because bodies come in varying lengths and widths, plan and measure carefully when buying, laying out, and cutting.** Buy enough panels for the front, back, and two sleeves. If available, purchase a matching ribbed band for finishing the neckline. Kits are packaged by specific garment and size. One labeled for an adult size may yield two children's sweaters; for a large men's size, you may need to buy two ladies' kits. **Caution:** Don't skimp on the number of panels or ribbed bands—these are primarily mill ends and manufacturers' overruns, so stock is limited with little chance for reorders. See Pattern Layout and Cutting, page 27, for how to handle the ribbing while cutting out.

Create-Your-Own Sweaterings

Knit or crochet your own sweater yardage, ribbing, or body by hand or machine. Or create small squares for a patchwork effect (see page 19). If you have the talent and time, advantages abound—an unlimited variety of color, fiber, weight, and stitch combinations is available. Knit the yardage as wide as the largest sweater piece and cut out. To avoid struggling with raveling and stretching, gauge for four or more stitches per inch.

Recyclables

Update or recut outdated or worn sweaters. Likely sources are your closets, rummage sales, and local thrift shops. Best bets would be long-lasting cashmeres, angoras, wools, and blends. Remember, women's and children's styles can be cut from larger men's sweaters. Salvage ribbing from an otherwise useless sweater.

Ribbing

Ribbing is rolled on a bolt and sold by the inch or yard (Fig. 2-3). Widths

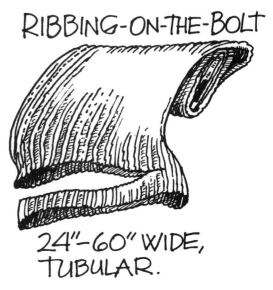

RIBBING-ON-THE-BOLT

24"–60" WIDE, TUBULAR.

Fig. 2-3

vary from 24" to 60", and fabric may be tubular or split open with selvages. Because there is no finished edge, ribbing must be applied double-layer. Test the stretch before choosing ribbing; some ribbing has great elasticity, while others simply stretch out and not back. No amount of sewing skill can offset poor-quality ribbing that stretches out of shape. **Note:** Self-fabric can also substitute for ribbing-by-the-yard, but resiliency is essential. If it's not resilient, binding or decoratively serging the edges might be a better option (see Binding the Edge, pages 32-33 or Decoratively Serged Edge Finish, page 30).

Ribbed Trim or Bands
(Fig. 2-4)

These ribbings all have one finished edge, allowing for single-layer application. Widths and lengths vary. If you need more resiliency and weight (such as when using 100% cotton), apply the

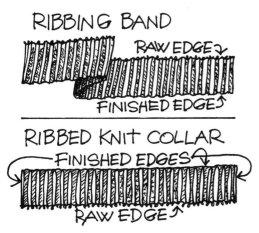

RIBBING BAND

RAW EDGE

FINISHED EDGES

RIBBED KNIT COLLAR

FINISHED EDGES

RAW EDGE

Fig. 2-4

ribbed trim double-layer, wrong sides together.

Ribbed Knit Collars
(Fig. 2-4)

Three sides are finished, so these can also be used as bands. Most collars are quite stable, so this material may not have the stretch and recovery required for cuffs. Test both the stretch and recovery.

Stretch Guidelines and Fit

Compare your sweatering to the stretch gauge on the back of the pattern envelope. On patterns designed for 25% stretch, 10" of the folded fabric must stretch to 12-1/2" in the true crosswise direction.

• **If your sweaterknit has less stretch than the pattern requires,** add 1/2" to the side seams and underarm sleeve seams. After fitting, trim away any excess seam-allowance width.

• **If your sweaterknit is much stretchier than called for** on the pattern gauge or in the fabric recommen-

dations, buy the pattern one size smaller, or simply take larger seam allowances after the first fitting.

• **Still uncertain about fit?** Compare the size and length of your pattern to a flattering ready-to-wear style made of sweatering with similar stretch and weight qualities.

Pattern Selection

All major pattern companies have joined knit specialty firms in offering sweater patterns. An alternative to buying a pattern is to trace one from a favorite ready-to-wear sweater (see Making Patterns from Ready-made Sweaters, pages 24 – 25).

• **Start with a simple design**—basic neckline, simple seaming, and smooth-capped, set-in, or raglan sleeves. A pullover is best for your first project; then graduate to a cardigan. Avoid darts and extra seams, and, for the fastest sewing, skip closures.

Corresponding straight seams on pattern pieces can be overlapped and eliminated. Convert center back and front seamlines to foldlines to save sewing time and minimize bulk. With few exceptions, curved side seams can be straightened; sweaterknit will contour to your figure without the help of contoured seams.

• **Streamline layout and cutting** by making full back and front pattern pieces (Fig. 2-5). Trace the pattern onto folded pattern paper, tissue, or non-woven interfacing. Then cut both layers for full pattern pieces.

• **Any style neckline**—crew, "V," turtleneck—**can be made from your**

PAPER FOLD

FOR EASIER LAYOUT & CUTTING, MAKE <u>FULL</u> BACK & FRONT BODICE PATTERNS OUT OF PATTERN PAPER, TISSUE OR NON-WOVEN INTER-FACING.

BACK

CENTER FRONT

FRONT

Fig. 2-5

basic pattern if it has a natural neck-line. For a natural neckline on your basic pattern, overlay any pattern with a natural back neckline (it will be noted on the back pattern piece if the neck-line is lower than natural). Trim the pattern seam allowance and trace this neckline on both the back and front pattern pieces. Then, for the front neckline shaping, trim away 2" at the center front, tapering to the shoulder seams, as shown (Fig. 2-6).

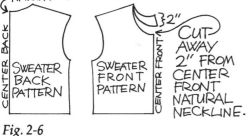

NATURAL BACK NECKLINE

CENTER BACK

SWEATER BACK PATTERN

SWEATER FRONT PATTERN

CENTER FRONT

2"

CUT AWAY 2" FROM CENTER FRONT NATURAL NECKLINE.

Fig. 2-6

Making Patterns from Ready-made Sweaters

You Have Two Options

Cut apart a worn style that you still treasure for its shape and fit, or trace around a favorite sweater while keeping it intact.

• **If cutting the sweater apart:** Trim off the ribbing, including a seam allowance, and recycle it for other sweater projects. Cut the sections apart along the seamlines (don't waste time pulling out stitches). Actually, you can use your serger for cutting sweaters apart; all cut edges will be finished and lay smoothly for tracing.

Fold the pattern paper or fabric and sweater in half lengthwise. Place the sweater pieces on the pattern material, as shown (Fig. 2-7), adding 1" seam and edge allowances throughout (later, before sewing ribbing to any edge, you will trim the edge to 3/8"). The wide allowances will both decrease stretching when serging and minimize ravel-ing that could weaken the seamlines. Transfer grainlines to the new pattern pieces.

USE CUT-APART SWEATER AS A PATTERN: ADD 1" ALLOWANCES ON TRACING PAPER.

Fig. 2-7

- **If using a sweater intact** (Fig. 2-8): Place each sweater section lengthwise,

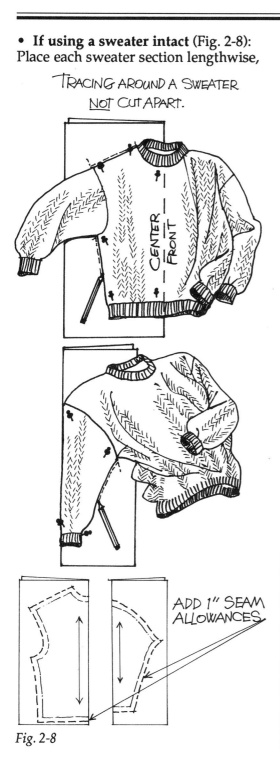

TRACING AROUND A SWEATER NOT CUT APART.

CENTER FRONT

ADD 1" SEAM ALLOWANCES

Fig. 2-8

as shown, on the folded pattern material. Add 1" seam allowances throughout (again, you will trim seams to 3/8" later, before applying ribbing). Transfer grainlines. Stretch the ribbing until the side seam is straight from the underarm to the bottom edge.

Timesaving Notions

✎ **Note:** For more notions information, refer to the general Timesaving Notions section in the Introduction and the Notions Guidelines for Specialty Fabrics chart on page *x*. Notions with fabric-specific explanations are explained here.

- **Scissors**

- **Pattern weights**

- **Machine needles**

- **Pins**—Avoid using pins as much as possible since they can easily become camouflaged in spongy sweatering. If you must pin, **use the longest pins with the largest colored heads.** Pin parallel to the seamline and remove them as you serge to avoid collisions with the knives or needle(s).

- **All-purpose or serger thread**

- **Woolly stretch nylon thread**

Interfacing

Less stable sweaterings can be stabilized by fusing a tricot interfacing, as shown, before or after cutting out (Fig. 2-9). Test-fuse first on fabric scraps. More fluid, sweater-like lines will form if the sweaterknit is not fused through-

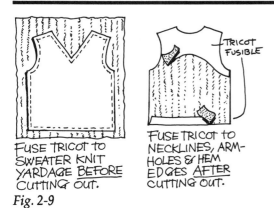

FUSE TRICOT to SWEATER KNIT YARDAGE BEFORE CUTTING OUT.

FUSE TRICOT to NECKLINES, ARM- HOLES & HEM EDGES AFTER CUTTING OUT.

Fig. 2-9

out, but the jacket-like fabric resulting from fusing is simple to seam and is ravel-proof. After testing, you may decide to limit fused stabilizing to sweater edges. Be careful not to flatten the sweater texture when fusing.

Fabric Preparation

Many sweaterings are labeled "needle-ready." Nonetheless, always prewash or steam the knit exactly as it will be laundered or cleaned later. **Ribbing bands, collars, and yardages to be used as trim should not be preshrunk**—the ribbing becomes difficult to manipulate and apply. One exception is if a dark or bright ribbing will be sewn to a lighter-shade sweatering; then prewashing will prevent unsightly bleeding of the dye. Also, steam sweaterknits to remove temporary creases.

✎ **Note:** Preshrinking compacts the knit structure, making the sweatering easier to handle and richer looking.

Cotton sweatering can become permanently creased. If the fabric is creased, refold it to avoid conspicuous placement. You'll prefer the texture,

resiliency, and shrink-free washability of cotton sweaterknits prewashed and dried by machine *twice*.

When knitting your own sweater yardage by machine, tube and block to stabilize stitches and control raveling. Tube by pulling the yardage several times along the lengthwise grain, holding opposite ends (Fig. 2-10). **If you have hand-knit or crocheted your sweatering, tubing is unnecessary**—proceed directly to blocking.

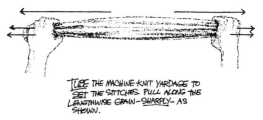

TUBE THE MACHINE-KNIT YARDAGE TO SET THE STITCHES. PULL ALONG THE LENGTHWISE GRAIN—SHARPLY—AS SHOWN.

Fig. 2-10

To block, pin the yardage to a flat, padded surface, wrong side up; a cutting board covered with a plaid wool or flannel helps keep the edges straight and prevents slippage when cutting later. Steam generously, but don't touch the iron to the knit. Move the steam back and forth in the crosswise direction. Allow to dry completely before handling or cutting out.

Pattern Layout and Cutting

• When cutting out sweatering, **follow the vertical knit for the lengthwise grainline.** The greater amount of stretch should go around the body. **Important:** Don't allow the knit fabric to hang over the edge of your cutting surface. Doing this will cause undesirable stretching and will distort the garment fit.

• **Professionals use weights to secure pattern pieces.** Pinning is slower, and pins can easily get lost in the sweater texture (and later damage serger knives). You'll also be less frustrated if you use long, sharp scissors for the fastest, smoothest strokes.

☞ **Special Tip: Allow 1" seams throughout.** The wider seam allowances will be quickly trimmed off as you serge and will substantially decrease stretched-out seams and edges.

• **Lay out the body pieces first, then the sleeves.** Match stripes, borders, or any other crosswise motif by matching the underarm of the body and sleeve pieces, as shown (Fig. 2-11).

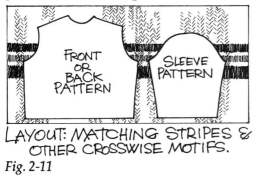

LAYOUT: MATCHING STRIPES & OTHER CROSSWISE MOTIFS.
Fig. 2-11

On sweater bodies with crosswise stripes or borders, you may find it impossible to match the sleeves to the body because of the knit-in ribbing edge. Choose a pattern with a very flat set-in sleeve cap (such as a dropped-shoulder style), where matching is not crucial. Or trim off the ribbing and resew it to the lower edge of the sleeves so that the motif matches across to the sweater bodice.

• **Sweater bodies call for special care and planning while laying out and cutting.** Double-check sleeve and body lengths before cutting. After cutting, lengthening a prefinished ribbed edge will be impossible. Place the pattern's finished length line along the finished edge of the knit-in ribbing. Before cutting, stretch the ribbed edge to form a straight line with the lengthwise rib of the side seam, as shown (Fig. 2-12).

STRETCH SWEATER BODY RIBBING & PIN INTO CUTTING BOARD.
Fig. 2-12

Use weights to secure, or pin into a cutting board. After cutting out, remove the weights or pins; the rib will spring back into the relaxed position. If ribbing will be sewn to the bottom edges, or if the edges will be hemmed or decoratively serged instead, **place the lower edge 1" from the top of the rib** (Fig. 2-13).

LAYOUT: WHEN RIBBING WILL BE SEWN ON, OR EDGE WILL BE HEMMED INSTEAD.
Fig. 2-13

Pressing

Avoid overhandling and over-pressing. Steam seams without pressing down on the knit. Only touch the fabric lightly. Instead, use your fingers to mold the area while the knit is still moist and warm. Take special care when steaming acrylic sweatering and ribbing; otherwise it will stretch out of shape.

Seams and Seam Finishes

Sweater seams should be stable. Don't necessarily assume that sweater seams will stretch with the fabric. But if the seams do stretch out, they won't stretch back. This causes ugly, wavy, bulky seams that overpower the silhouette and relegate your creation to the ranks of regrettably "homemade." Follow these guidelines for the fastest, most subtle seaming:

• **Adjust for the widest stitch width and a medium to long length.** The bulkier the sweatering, the longer the stitch length should be to prevent stretching.

• To further minimize stretching, **lighten the pressure on the presser foot** (refer to your owner's manual).

• Keep in mind that **the more unstable your sweaterknit, the more stable the seam should be.** For example, on loosely constructed knits and hand-knits, straight-stitch seams first, then trim off the excess seam allowance with a 2- or 3-thread finish. See Fig. 2-14 for reference.

• **Do not stretch the fabric as you sew or serge.**

• **Use the differential feed on your serger** (not available on all models—consult your manual or ask your dealer). This mechanism can effectively control stretching of sweater seams and edges. There are two sets of feed dogs—one set in front of the

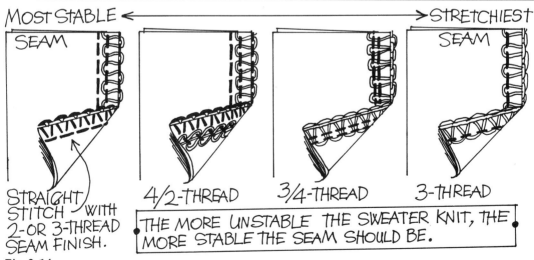

MOST STABLE ←   → STRETCHIEST
SEAM   SEAM

STRAIGHT STITCH WITH 2-OR 3-THREAD SEAM FINISH.   4/2-THREAD   3/4-THREAD   3-THREAD

THE MORE UNSTABLE THE SWEATER KNIT, THE MORE STABLE THE SEAM SHOULD BE.

Fig. 2-14

presser foot and one behind. Set the differential feed dial on 2.0; the front set of feed dogs will feed the fabric into the serger twice as fast as the rear feed dogs release it. This process eases the fabric into the machine and prevents stretching. Get similar results without the differential feed by **force-feeding the fabric into the machine while holding the layers against the back of the presser foot.**

• **Alternate seam-allowance directions at intersections to minimize bulk and ensure jam-free serging.**

Stabilizing Seams and Edges

• **With the exception of shoulder seams, most sweater seams won't need extra stabilization.** To stabilize shoulder seams, serge over bias tricot strips, stretching the tricot as you serge (Fig. 2-15). This will stabilize the seam in the relaxed position. Or serge over stay tape or a lining selvage strip. Measure the stabilizer on the seamline of the **pattern piece** and mark that length (rather than using the stretch-prone sweater shoulder seam as a guide). Place the stabilizer on the front shoulder seam and serge, catching it under the stitches.

Also, try substituting clear polyurethane elastic for the other stabilizers recommended. Cut to length and serge in place as instructed above.

• **For flat, smooth shoulder seams (best for shoulder pads), straight-stitch, right sides together,** and press open (Fig. 2-15). Then topstitch at 1/4" on both sides of the seamline, through the seam allowances.

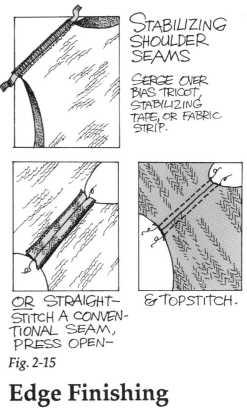

STABILIZING SHOULDER SEAMS

SERGE OVER BIAS TRICOT, STABILIZING TAPE, OR FABRIC STRIP.

OR STRAIGHT-STITCH A CONVEN-TIONAL SEAM, PRESS OPEN—

& TOPSTITCH.

Fig. 2-15

Edge Finishing

Ribbing Edge-Finish

Most sweater seamsters prefer finishing edges with ribbing because it is the fastest, easiest, and most like ready-to-wear. Ribbing is usually cut smaller than the edge to be finished so that it will hug the body and control stretching. **Use only the best, most resilient ribbing; stretched-out ribbing ruins the look, fit, and comfort even of a well-sewn sweater.**

Handling sweater ribbing is a little trickier than T-shirt ribbing because of the wide variety of textures, weights, and stretch characteristics. With few exceptions, **avoid cotton ribbing-by-the-yard and choose instead the more resilient cotton ribbed bands and use**

them double-layer. Here are some more helpful hints:

• Choose ribbing that is compatible in weight, fiber, and care to the sweater fabric.

• **Before applying the ribbing, trim the seam allowances of both the ribbing and sweating to 3/8".** Narrower seam allowances are much easier to work with when serging.

• On necklines which require stretchability (for putting the sweater on and taking it off), use 3- or 3/4-thread serging.

• **Lengthen serger stitches.** When the ribbing relaxes, the stitches will compact, increasing thread density and bulk. Also, **the more thread covering the seams, the more the ribbing will stretch out permanently.** Seam width should be about 5mm.

• **Always sew with the ribbing on top.** Usually, the more the ribbing is stretched, the more it will curve. However, many sweater ribbings are soft, with poor recovery power, so **ease the sweating to fit the ribbing rather than stretching the ribbing to fit the edge.** Never stretch the sweating when applying the ribbing; it will remain stretched out.

• **To prevent mismatched seams at the bottom edge of ribbed cuffs or side seams, stretch the ribbing taut,** as shown (Fig. 2-16). Stretch it the most at the cuff side seam.

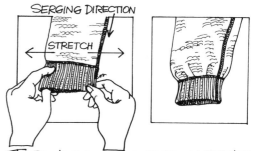

TO PREVENT RIBBED CUFF SEAM MISMATCH.

Fig. 2-16

Decoratively Serged Edge Finish

Decoratively serged edges are lovely but less stable than those rib-finished. To compensate:

• Cut facings of more-stable jersey or doubleknit, then serge-finish through the fabric and facing layers.

• Serge over pearl cotton, yarn, or elastic thread, being careful not to catch it in the stitches. Pull up the yarn or thread to ease the edge to the correct shape and size. For a neckline, try on the garment to make sure it will fit over your head.

• Fuse strips of tricot interfacing to the wrong side of the edges, then serge.

Use either a 2- or 3-thread stitch for decorative finishing. Most applications, but not all, feature the decorative thread or yarn in the upper looper only (it has the least number of guides for easier feeding, plus the decorative thread will show from the top side). Adjust for the widest stitch and begin testing with the longest length, shortening in small increments to achieve the proper coverage without stretching the edge. **The heavier the thread or yarn, the looser the specific tension will need to be;** some decorative threads feed most smoothly if you bypass the tension dial altogether.

Before beginning to serge, turn the handwheel to ensure smooth feeding and correct stitch formation. For the most accurate test, use scraps of the actual sweater fabric, optimally cut on the same grain as the edge to be finished. **Serge** *slowly* **while testing and adjusting machine settings.**

When using decorative threads or yarns, consider this: If the yarn is too thick or nubby to feed smoothly through the guides and looper eye, and if the sweatering isn't too heavy, you can flatlock yarn strand(s) to the fabric surface. Flatlocked stitching can be either decorative or made "invisible" by using monofilament nylon thread. For a coordinated edge, simply serge over the matching yarn strand(s) with monofilament nylon thread.

Fast Hems

To hem sweatering (Fig. 2-17):

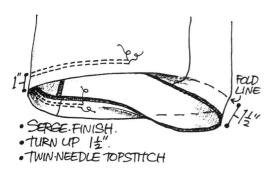

- SERGE·FINISH.
- TURN UP 1½".
- TWIN·NEEDLE TOPSTITCH

Fig. 2-17

1. Serge-finish the hem edge using either a differential feed or by force-feeding the fabric into the machine.

2. Turn up the finished edge 1-1/2" and topstitch with a twin needle 1" from the hemline.

Special Techniques

Steps to a Speedy Crew

1. **Cut the ribbing to the proper length and width.** The greatest stretch should go around your head. For a 1-1/4" finished width, cut ribbing or ribbed bands to be applied double-layer 3-1/4" wide (twice the finished width plus 5/8" seam allowances). Ribbed bands to be applied single-layer can be cut 1-5/8" wide (the finished width plus a seam allowance). Straight-stitch the bands, right sides together, into a circle (Fig. 2-18).

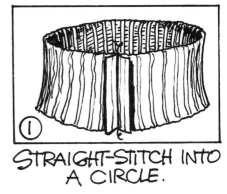

STRAIGHT-STITCH INTO A CIRCLE.

Fig. 2-18

2. Fold the ribbing circle, wrong sides together, and quartermark with long pins (Fig. 2-19).

FOLD WRONG SIDES TOGETHER & ¼-MARK.

Fig. 2-19

3. Quartermark the neckline and match it to the ribbing, right sides together. The quartermarks will usually fall in front of the shoulder seams (Fig. 2-20).

¼-MARK NECKLINE & MATCH TO RIBBING.

Fig. 2-20

4. Serge-seam with the ribbing on top (Fig. 2-21).

Or for ribbed crew applications on lighter-weight sweaterings, **try this factory method** (Fig. 2-22):

1. Serge one shoulder seam.

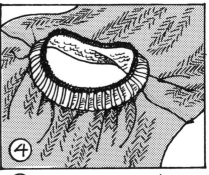

SERGE WITH THE RIBBING ON TOP.

Fig. 2-21

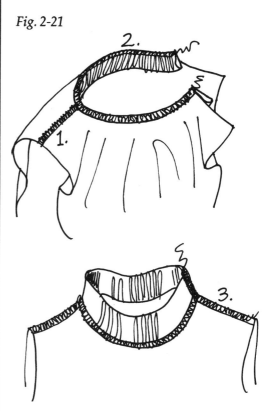

Fig. 2-22

2. Serge the ribbing to the neckline.

3. Serge the other shoulder seam, sewing through the crew ribbing at the

neckline. On most fabrics, it is easiest to start serging the seam at the armhole edge. Weave the thread ends back through the serged seam.

Binding the Edge

Use ribbing-by-the-yard or self-fabric to bind the edge (Fig. 2-23). An

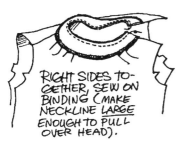

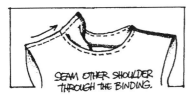

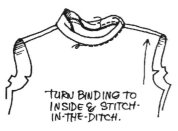

Fig. 2-23

inherent advantage of this binding is that the neckline or edge will never stretch out. The finished binding should be no wider than 1"; cut crosswise strips three times the finished binding width plus 1/2". Serge-finish one long edge before applying. For a neckline application:

1. **Straight-stitch one shoulder seam and press it open.**

2. Right sides together, **straight-stitch the binding to the edge.** The seam allowance should be the width of the finished trim. Stretch slightly around curves so that the binding will lie flat. Try the bound edge over your head, pinning the other shoulder seam. (It should be large enough to pull on and off easily.)

3. Straight-stitch the other shoulder seam, through the binding, and press it open. Trim the shoulder seam bulk.

4. Turn the serge-finished edge of the binding to the inside. (The binding should be an even width throughout.)

5. Stitch-in-the-ditch to secure the binding in place.

Deep Lapped "V"
(Fig. 2-24)

Follow these steps for a deep lapped "V." You'll be guaranteed an even width and a smooth-fitting neckline finish every time.

1. **Measure the "V" depth and ribbing width carefully.** Remember, the finished ribbing width will fill the "V"; cut down the "V" proportionately. The V-point seamline on most ready-made tops is positioned about 3" to 5" below the bustline (Fig. 2-24). The finished ribbing width is usually 3" to 4"; cut to allow 1/4" seam(s) and double the width if using ribbing-by-the-yard rather than a ribbed band. The ribbing length should be 3" longer than the cut edge of the neckline. To better estimate how much to trim away for the V-neckline, cut out the top with a shallow

DEEP CROSS-OVER "V" NECKLINE.
LAPPED

Fig. 2-24

"V," seam the shoulders, and pin-baste the ribbing in place; then try on the garment. **Caution:** If you plan to wear the top without a shirt underneath, be careful not to cut the "V" too low, which could make it inappropriate for daytime or office dressing.

2. Serge the shoulder seams.

3. Stay-stitch 2" on either side of the "V" point. Begin stitching at the center front and stitch up the left side; repeat for the right side.

4. Pin the ribbing to the right side of the neckline, stretching slightly and allowing 1" for lapping at the center front (Fig. 2-25). With the garment on

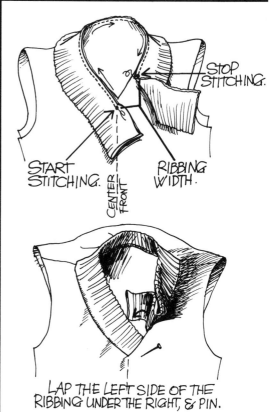

LAP THE LEFT SIDE OF THE RIBBING UNDER THE RIGHT, & PIN.

Fig. 2-25

top, straight-stitch from the center front to the right shoulder seam. Stretch the ribbing more between the shoulder seams (it should be about two-thirds of the back neckline measurement), pin, and stitch, distributing the ease evenly.

5. Pin the ribbing to the left side of the neckline, stretching slightly. Stop stitching before you reach the "V" point and leave an opening equal to the finished ribbing width measurement.

6. Lay the top on a flat surface, right side up. Tuck the ribbing inside, lapping the left side under the right. Adjust and pin until smooth and flat. Try on the garment to check the fit.

7. From the wrong side, straight-stitch the opening closed. Pivot at the "V" point and secure the underlap to the right seam allowance. After checking the "V" fit, serge to neaten and add durability.

Wide Mitered "V"
(Fig. 2-26)

When ribbing is 4" to 7" wide, it becomes an integral part of the garment shape. Take advantage of novelty ribbings and contrasting colors for this wide mitered "V"—the angles draw attention to the face and shoulders, thereby creating the illusion of a slimmer waist and hips.

WIDE MITERED "V" RIBBING.

Fig. 2-26

1. See Deep Lapped "V" on page 33, Step 1.

2. Serge one shoulder seam. Beginning at the unseamed shoulder, serge the ribbing to the neckline with the ribbing on top. Just before you reach the "V," pull the sweater fabric so that both sides of the "V" are in a straight line under the ribbing. As described in Steps 4 and 5 of the Deep Lapped "V," stretch the ribbing slightly on the left and right front edges, and more (about a 2:3 ratio) along the back neckline.

3. Serge the other shoulder seam, through the ribbing.

4. Miter the "V" by folding it in half, as shown (Fig. 2-27). Pin-baste from the top-center-front foldline to the ribbing edge; try on the garment. Adjust the seam so that the garment fits smoothly at the neckline and across the bustline.

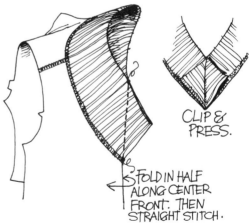

CLIP & PRESS.

FOLD IN HALF ALONG CENTER FRONT. THEN STRAIGHT STITCH.

Fig. 2-27

5. Stitch from the ribbing seam to the ribbing edges, taking care to align the seams and edges accurately. Clip the miter fold and press back. Hand-tack or straight-stitch the raw edges of the ribbing to the seams.

Altering Sweaters

• **Try the sweater on inside-out.** Use large safety pins to adjust the fit (Fig. 2-28). (Straight pins can easily get lost in the thick sweatering or fall out of loosely knit textures.) **Key alterations:** Shorten the bodice and/or take in the side seams and sleeve underarms.

Fig. 2-28

👉 **Special Tip:** Shoulder pads instantly update any sweater. Fit the sweater with the pads in place. If you don't have pads for the sweater, make an interchangeable pair that you can wear with a number of outfits.

Shorten a Sweater:

Begin by cutting off the knit-in ribbing, allowing a 1" seam allowance (Fig. 2-29). Cut the sweater to the desired length, leaving a 1" seam allowance on the bodice. Match the

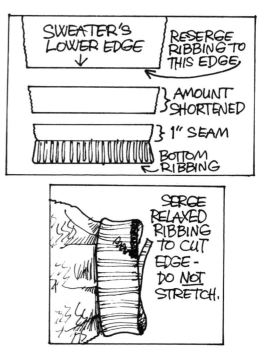

Fig. 2-29

midpoints and side seams of the ribbing and the bodice. With the ribbing on top, re-serge it to the bodice, stitching next to (but not through) the ribbing. Ribbing should be sewn on in the relaxed position, not stretched out; the bodice will automatically ease to fit the ribbing.

✎ **Note:** When shortening the sweater moves the ribbing closer to the waistline, you may need to take it in. Take deeper seam(s) in the ribbing before reapplying it to the sweater bodice.

Convert a Turtleneck to a Johnny Collar:

This is the popular crew/collar combination. You must have a deeper turtleneck (5" minimum) for this conversion; a 6" turtleneck will produce a 1-1/4" crew. Slit the turtleneck down the center front to within 4" of the seam. Pull the slit to form a straight line as you serge-finish the raw edge; turn 1/4" to the right side (Fig. 2-30) and topstitch. Fold the turtleneck to the wrong side to form a 1-1/4"- to 1-1/2"-wide crew. Then stitch-in-the-ditch to secure the crew portion of the collar. Fold the remaining turtleneck fabric back over the crew to form the collar.

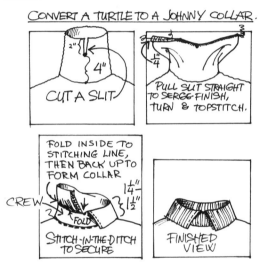

Fig. 2-30

Convert a Turtleneck to a Crew:

Simply fold the turtleneck down (inside) to the desired width and pin. If necessary, trim off some of the turtleneck width so that the narrower crew width will lie flat. Serge over the original seamline to secure.

Revitalize Stretched-Out Ribbing:

First, cut off the ribbing, then take a deeper side seam in the ribbing and reapply it to the edge. Or replace stretched-out ribbing with ribbing that is more resilient. Because color matching is nearly impossible, strive for an attractive contrast.

Easiest Serging Order
(Fig. 2-31)

When assembling your sweater, serge using the flat method of construction for the easiest handling and most accurate stitching:

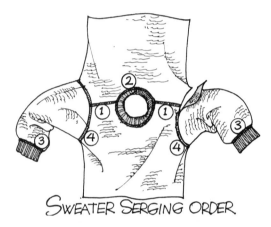

Fig. 2-31

1. Serge the shoulder seams. Press the seams toward the back.

2. Sew the ribbing into a circle and serge it to the neckline. Do not stretch the ribbing; instead, ease the sweatering to fit.

3. Serge the ribbing to the bottom of the sleeves.

4. Serge the sleeves to the bodice armholes.

☞ **Special Tips: When serging the sleeves to the garment, sew with the sleeve cap down and the bodice on**

top (Fig. 2-32). Ease the sleeve to the armhole rather than stretching the armhole to the sleeve. Distribute the ease along the whole edge to prevent a gathered look at the top of the cap.

Fig. 2-32

5. Starting at the lower edge of the bodice, serge one side seam, continuing through the sleeve underarm and cuff (Fig. 2-33).

6. Serge the ribbing to the bottom edge of the sweater (Fig. 2-33). This may be the most important tip in this chapter: **Serge the ribbing to the bottom edge in the relaxed, not stretched-out, position. Sew with the ribbing on top, easing the sweater edge underneath.** If you stretch the ribbing while serging along this crosswise edge, it will assume the stretched-out position permanently.

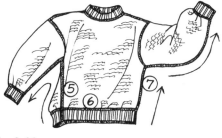

Fig. 2-33

7. Serge the remaining side seam in the same manner as described in Step 5 (Fig. 2-33). Weave the thread ends back through the serged seam.

Quick Tips

• To prevent raveling, serge-finish fabric edges before pretreating.

• Ripping is seldom necessary. **Just trim off the original stitching with the serger knives** (Fig. 2-34).

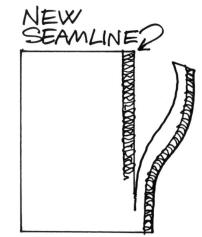

Fig. 2-34

• After sewing the shoulder seams, try on the garment to make sure it will fit over your head. **Trim away in 1/8" increments until the neckline pulls on and off with ease. Children's head sizes are larger in proportion to their bodies than adults, so fit first.**

• To make a mock-turtleneck for the sweater, **cut the ribbing 7" wide** and apply as for the crewneck.

Project: Quick-and-Easy Sweater

Select 1-1/2 yards of 54"- or 60"-wide sweatering and 14" of coordinating or matching ribbing.

Neckline—3-1/4" wide by 2/3 of the neckline opening.

Lower edge—7" wide by 3/4 the lower edge opening.

Sleeves—2 strips 7" wide by arm circumference.

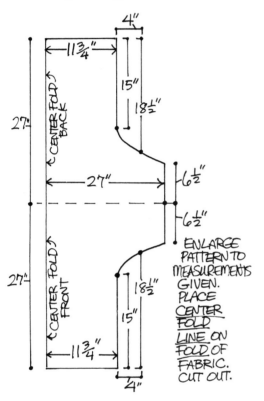

Fig. 2-35

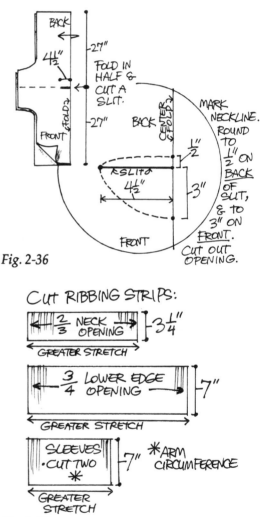

Fig. 2-36

1. **Cut a sweater from the yardage using the measurements as shown** (Fig. 2-35).

2. Fold the fabric in half lengthwise and cut the neck opening, as shown (Fig. 2-36).

3. **Cut ribbing strips** as follows (Fig. 2-37):

Fig. 2-37

4. **Apply the ribbing as for the crewneck and serge with the fast serging order, page 37, eliminating shoulder and sleeve seams.**

3. Quick and Easy Stretch Fashions

Sportswear and casual clothes made from *Lycra*-blend stretch fabrics are easily and professionally sewn with the serger. The best ready-to-wear techniques for seaming and finishing can be quickly copied by serging. Overlock stitches stretch with the fabric for optimum comfort and fit.

Fabric Choices

Lycra

Lycra, **DuPont's spandex product, is an elastic fiber that is easily combined with other natural or man-made fibers** to make a uniquely stretchy and resilient fabric. Lightweight and durable, the amount of *Lycra* dictates the degree of stretch in a fabric: the more *Lycra,* the more stretch. Check the end of the bolt or the label—20% *Lycra* will give a lot of stretch to the fabric, while 4% will add little stretch.

Nylon/*Lycra*

Nylon blended with *Lycra* has long been the knit of choice for swimwear. Now nylon/*Lycras* are equally popular for aerobics, running, cycling, dancing, skiing, and skating. When shopping, note that *Antron/Lycra* blends are nylon/*Lycra*-blends; *Antron* is one of DuPont's brands of nylon fibers.

Nylon lends bright color and shiny finish to the fabric blend. Other advantages? Durability, easy care, super-quick drying, and good availability of the solids and prints seen in best-selling ready-to-wear designs.

Nylon/*Lycra* is sold in different weights and is indicated by ounces per yard. Heaviest nylon/*Lycras* (8 to 12 ounces) are recommended for skiwear and inserts in wovens. Medium weights (5 to 8 ounces) can be used for bicycle shorts or swimwear. Lightest weights (5 ounces or less) are perfect for running or dancing tights, leotards that will be worn in layers, and for swimsuit linings. Let personal preference guide your selection.

Check out sportswear and lingerie departments. **You'll find a new breed of nylon/*Lycra*-blend stretch knits: heavier, beefier,** nearly as resilient as the power net used for girdles (Fig. 3-1). Because of weight, enhanced durability, and stretch control, this new fabric is found in sport and exercise bras and tank tops, racing shorts, and pant-like tights. It's now available to the home-sewing market, primarily through knit specialty retailers and mail order.

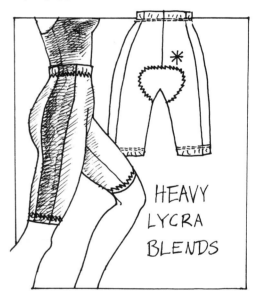

Fig. 3-1

These heavier *Lycra*-blends offer the same body-revealing fit, comfort, and easy care of their lighter-weight counterparts. **Greater support is their newfound appeal.** Also, because of their heavier weight, these knits are warmer and more durable, popular for ice skating, running, walking, and cycling.

The fiber blend and stretchability will vary from fabric to fabric. **Most of** the heavier *Lycra*-blends are Raschel knits with one-way stretch in the lengthwise direction and very little, if any, in the crosswise direction. Because most actionwear patterns are designed for two-way stretch fabrics, pattern alterations must compensate for the one-way stretch (see Pattern Layout and Cutting, pages 46 – 48).

✎ **Note:** Most of these fabrics embossed with metallics are not treated for protection from saltwater.

Cotton/*Lycra*

When *Lycra* is blended with cotton or cotton/polyester, it **has a matte finish which is more absorbent than when blended with nylon and more comfortable to wear.** Cotton/*Lycras* are at least as stretchy (or more so) as nylon/*Lycra* blends but they don't dry as quickly. Cotton/*Lycras* are widely available in a variety of solids and prints. For breathability and absorption, choose cotton/*Lycras* for tops and leotards. For fastest drying and a leaner look, choose nylon/*Lycras* for tights, shorts, and leggings (narrow pants).

Textured *Lycra*-Blends

Some nylon/*Lycra* and cotton/*Lycra* blend knits are textured or puckered. Compare the stretch of these fabrics to the stretch chart on the pattern; **puckering, in particular, can enhance stretchability.**

☞ **Special Tip:** If you're the modest type, try one of the puckered *Lycra*-blends for swimwear. The bubbled surface texture is less revealing than plain-surfaced, unlined knits

(which, when wet, can be like wearing no swimsuit at all!).

Selecting Stretch Fabrics

Stretch fabric provides comfort for the wearer and the stretchability required for movement and a snug fit. Consider the following information when making selections:

• *Lycra*-blend knit may be 45" or 60" wide.

• **Most patterns are designed for knits that stretch in both the crosswise and lengthwise directions.** These fabrics are called two-way or four-way stretch knits (Fig. 3-2). (It's rather confusing, but two-way stretch means the same as four-way stretch.) If you choose a pattern that specifies two-way or four-way stretch knit, it is imperative that you use this fabric type; otherwise the finished garment will not fit.

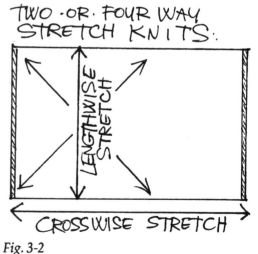

Fig. 3-2

• **Stretch varies from fabric to fabric, so check the ratio of stretch;** compare it to the requirements on the back of the pattern envelope before buying. If the stretch is different, you will need to make alterations in the pattern to compensate and achieve the desired fit. *Lycra*-**blended fabrics usually (but not always) stretch 50 to 100% in the lengthwise, crosswise, and bias directions.**

• Two-way (or four-way) stretch knits are snag-resistant and will not run.

• Metallic-embossed fabrics have less stretch than solids or prints.

Gauging the Stretch Ratio

To determine the stretch ratio of the fabric, stretch 4" of fabric folded in the crosswise direction, then stretch 4" of the fabric folded in the lengthwise direction. **If the folded fabric easily stretches to 6", it has 50% stretch. If it stretches easily to 8", it has 100% stretch** (Fig. 3-3).

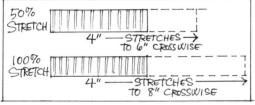

Fig. 3-3

Pattern Selection

Most pattern companies offer swim- and actionwear patterns in a wide range of sizes and designs. (Check with your local fabric store or machine dealer or see the Fabrics-by-Mail Directory at the end of the book.)

• Select most patterns according to bust size. Choose patterns for tights and shorts by hip size.

• **Choose a pattern designed especially for two-way (or four-way) stretch fabric.** Match the fabric stretchability to the pattern stretch ratio for the best fit. (Most garments are undersized for a stretched fit, so adequate fabric stretch is mandatory.) For a bust size different than hip size, choose a multisized pattern. Follow the cutting lines for both and blend the lines together.

• **Follow pattern instructions to make adjustments for fit.** Many one-piece actionwear patterns will give an overall body measurement chart on which the pattern is based. Take your overall body measurement as shown in the pattern, compare it to the chart, and make the appropriate adjustments on the pattern's shorten and lengthen lines. **Because it is an overall measurement, the overall adjustment will have to be divided and made uniformly on both the back and front shorten and lengthen lines.** Refer to your pattern guidesheet.

• **If in doubt about measurements, make the garment longer.** If it is too long, straps can be shortened or the bottom can be recut. **For adjustments to the height of the leg,** see page 56.

Timesaving Notions

✎ **Note:** For more notions information, refer to the general Timesaving Notions section in the Introduction and the Notions Guidelines for Specialty Fabrics chart on page x. Notions with fabric-specific explanations are explained here.

- Scissors or a rotary cutter and mat
- Pattern weights
- Machine needles
- Twin-needles—Use a twin needle in your sewing machine for hemming, topstitching, and encasing elastic finishes (Fig. 3-4). Use a new sharp needle, size 2.0/80 or 3.0/90, to avoid skipped stitches and holes in the fabric.

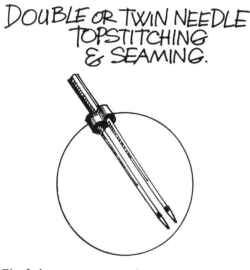

DOUBLE OR TWIN NEEDLE TOPSTITCHING & SEAMING.

Fig. 3-4

- Pins
- All-purpose or serger thread
- Woolly stretch nylon
- Marking Pen
- Elastics—Elastic is an essential element of stretch fashion. It stabilizes and finishes neckline, arm, and leg openings, plus it reinforces stretch belts and straps.

Elastic Tips

For any stretch-knit garment, pick

an elastic fabricated specifically for swimwear, one that is chlorine-resistant and will retain its stretch-ability when wet and stitched through. Swimwear elastic resists deterioration and is long-lasting. (This elastic can be used on all garments, not just for swimwear.)

Several types of swimwear elastic are available (Fig. 3-5):

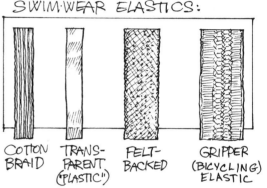

SWIM·WEAR ELASTICS:

COTTON BRAID — TRANS-PARENT ("PLASTIC") — FELT-BACKED — GRIPPER (BICYCLING) ELASTIC

Fig. 3-5

- **Cotton/spandex braid elastic**—Can be stitched through easily without stretching out. It is available in several widths, but the 1/4", 3/8", and 3/4" widths are the most widely used for actionwear.

- **Transparent elastic** (not to be con-fused with rubber elastic)—Can also be stitched through without stretching out. Available in 1/8", 1/4", 3/8", 1/2", and 3/4" widths, this 100% polyure-thane elastic is impervious to chlorine, although it may discolor (which isn't a problem because it doesn't show). Many ready-to-wear manufacturers use it because it is thin, which encour-ages sewability and discourages bulk.

- **Felt-backed polyester/spandex elastic**—Favored for finishing the edges of bandeaus because it is soft next to the skin. It is available in various widths, but the more stable 3/4" width is most often used for this purpose.

• **Gripper (or bicycling) polyester/ spandex elastic**—This lightweight, braided elastic has one rubberized side. Sold in shades of black and white and 1" widths. Because the rubberized side prevents creeping, it is popular for finishing the leg openings of bicycling-style shorts.

Lining

• **Special nylon swim linings are available in basic white, nude, and black.** Nude works well for most fabric colors because it blends with most skin colors.

• Always line the crotch area. Self-fabric can be used for the crotch lining if swim lining is not available.

• **For lining the crotch area** of leotards, shorts, or tights, use **a lightweight 100% cotton singleknit.**

• **Light-colored swim fabrics are translucent when wet, so consider lining the front and possibly the back of the suit.** Self-fabric or a lighter-weight *Lycra*-blend knit can also be used if it is solid-colored.

• For maximum support and modesty, line with self-fabric, making sure a print will not show through from the right side.

• Many patterns include lining patterns and instructions. If your pattern doesn't, **cut the lining from the swimsuit pattern.** Linings are two-way

stretch fabrics, but they vary in stretchability. **Select a lining with the same amount of stretch as the swimsuit fabric.** (Or, if it has less stretch, compensate by adding to the length and width of the pattern piece.) If the lining has more stretch, no adjustment is necessary. Swim lining can also be partial; for instance, only across the bust to add soft support and a modesty layer.

Easy Stretch Lining Technique

This lining technique will keep the fabric and lining from shifting and conceal the seam allowances from both the right and wrong sides of the garment.

✎ **Note:** If your pattern has a separate crotch piece, then serge the garment crotch to the back of the garment and the lining crotch to the back of the lining.

1. Place the garment pieces to be seamed right sides together. Then place the lining pieces to be seamed right sides together.

2. Place the two lining pieces onto the two garment pieces with the garment back and lining back wrong sides together, matching the cut edges. Serge-seam the side, shoulder, and crotch through all layers, as shown (Fig. 3-6).

3. Turn the layers right-side out through the neck or leg opening so that the seam is concealed between the layers.

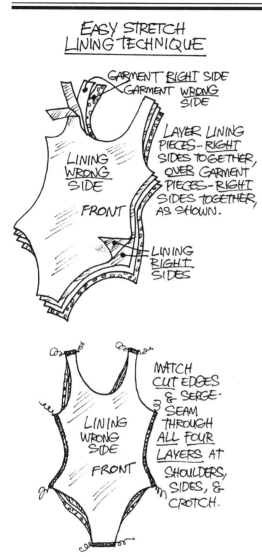

EASY STRETCH LINING TECHNIQUE

GARMENT <u>RIGHT</u> SIDE
GARMENT <u>WRONG</u> SIDE

LINING WRONG SIDE

FRONT

LAYER LINING PIECES - RIGHT SIDES TOGETHER, OVER GARMENT PIECES - RIGHT SIDES TOGETHER, AS SHOWN.

LINING RIGHT SIDES

LINING WRONG SIDE

FRONT

MATCH CUT EDGES & SERGE. SEAM THROUGH ALL FOUR LAYERS AT SHOULDERS, SIDES, & CROTCH.

Fig. 3-6

Fabric Preparation

Lycra-blended fabrics have minimal shrinkage, whereas cottons shrink up to 1" per yard. **Pretreat fabrics as you would the finished garment by machine washing and line or drip drying** (laundering will also help to eliminate skipped stitches). Do not pretreat the elastics. Stitching through the elastics compensates for any shrinkage.

Pattern Layout and Cutting

Layout Tips

• **Most garments are cut so that the greatest stretch goes** around **the body** (crosswise on the pattern). **With tights, the greater stretch should be** vertical, **up and down the leg** (Fig. 3-7).

FOR BEST FIT:

GREATEST STRETCH DIRECTION

Fig. 3-7

• Check the stretch of the fabric—in nylon/*Lycra*, the greatest stretch often, but not always, parallels the length of the fabric. When laying out the pattern, **you may have to refold the fabric so the stretch will go around the body in the finished garment** (Fig. 3-8).

• Then follow the pattern layout. Check the direction and placement of all one-way or engineered prints and

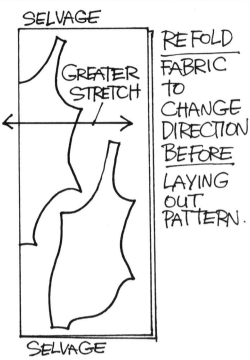

SELVAGE

GREATER
STRETCH

REFOLD
FABRIC
TO
CHANGE
DIRECTION
BEFORE
LAYING
OUT
PATTERN.

SELVAGE

Fig. 3-8

napped textures. **Do not allow the fabric to hang over the cutting table** or it may stretch, altering the fit of the finished garment.

Cutting Tips

• Use the "with nap" layout because stretch fabric has a napped surface. If necessary, ignore the "with nap" layout to achieve the desired print placement.

• **Cotton/Lycra-blends may have a permanent crease running lengthwise on the fabric.** Steam-press the fabric lightly to try to remove the crease. If this doesn't work, refold the fabric to cut away from the fold, or position it inconspicuously.

• Cut the lining with the greatest

stretch going around the body, just like the outer fabric.

• Two-way stretch fabrics can be cut on the bias (to make chevron stripes or to yield more length) without altering the fit.

• Most activewear patterns have 1/4" seam allowances. **Widen seam allowances if you're unsure of the fit.** Also, when marking the notches, use an erasable marking pen (do NOT clip into the seam allowances).

• When cutting, use your sharpest shears to avoid snags or pulled threads in the fabric.

• Cut the elastic later, when serging and sewing.

Two-way stretch designs will require fit alterations to compensate if you are using the heavier one-way stretch fabric (see pages 41 – 42). Here's how:

1. **The greater stretch should be placed** around **the body.** On tight patterns designed for two-way stretch fabrics, the stretch is usually vertical;

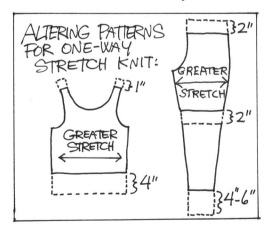

ALTERING PATTERNS
FOR ONE-WAY
STRETCH KNIT:

31"

GREATER
STRETCH

32"

GREATER
STRETCH

32"

GREATER
STRETCH

34"

34"-6"

Fig. 3-9

change the layout direction so the stretch goes around the body.

2. Add length to pattern pieces to compensate for minimal vertical stretch (Fig. 3-9). **For bra tops, add 1" to straps and 4" to the lower edge** on both the front and back pattern pieces. **For tights and shorts, add 2" in length at the waist edge. Add 2" to shorts and 4" – 6" to tights at the bottom edge.**

Seams and Seam Finishes

Movement places stress on all stretch-fabric seams, so they must give. **A 3- or 3/4-thread serged seam provides the necessary stretch.** A 4/2-thread chainstitch/overedge combination can be used, but this requires stretching as you serge (Fig. 3-10).

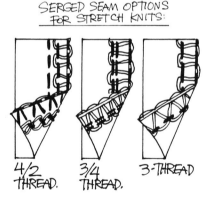

SERGED SEAM OPTIONS FOR STRETCH KNITS:

4/2 THREAD. 3/4 THREAD. 3-THREAD

MOST STABLE SEAM ⟷ STRETCHIEST SEAM

Fig. 3-10

Stitch Settings

Use a medium to wide width (3.5 to 5mm) and a medium to long length (3 to 4mm).

Tension Settings

Adjust to a balanced-tension stitch and test. Serge parallel to the stretchiest grain direction. Stretch the seamline rigorously. **If the seam breaks, loosen the needle thread tension.** (If a thread breaks, it will most likely be the needle thread.) If the needle thread continues to break under the stress of pulling, hold the fabric taut or stretch slightly while serging.

Securing Seam Ends

This is usually unnecessary because seam ends will be reinforced by intersecting conventionally sewn straight-stitching. To secure seams in actionwear garments, thread the chain back into serged stitching. Using seam sealant in these close-fitting garments may cause skin irritation.

Matching Stripes or Design Lines

When beginning to serge, allow the bottom seam allowance (the one next to the feed dogs) to extend slightly past the upper layer so that you can see to match layers. Perfect matching every time!

Fitting

• To fit, **try on the garment before applying the elastic.** (Elastic will add stability to the edges but isn't needed to fit the garment.) If a one-piece garment, such as a swimsuit or leotard, is too long, **shorten the shoulder straps and recut the neckline** (Fig. 3-11).

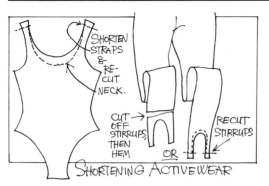

Fig. 3-11

• For tights, **fit before finishing the stirrups** at the lower edge. If too long, recut the stirrups or cut the stirrups off and simply hem (see Fast Hems and Finishes, page 55).

• **If the garment is too large,** take 1/4" deeper seams, incrementally, until you achieve the right fit. **If the garment is too small,** the narrow seam allowances narrow your alternatives—can you insert a racing stripe of stretch fabric in the side seams?

Elastic Edge Finishing

Cutting Guidelines

• **Cut elastic during construction, as it is needed.** (Follow the pattern instructions for determining length.) Some patterns include elastic cutting guides (alter the guides if you've altered the fit); other patterns require measuring the openings and then cutting accordingly. Refer to the ratios given in the pattern or, if not given, follow the guidelines below.

• In general, **for leg openings, apply the elastic to the front leg opening in a 1:1 ratio (or 1" less) and to the back**

leg opening with 2" to 4" less than the opening measurement. This will make it cling to the derrière contour, preventing it from riding up (Fig. 3-12). The higher the leg cut, the greater the elastic-to-fabric stretch ratio across the back leg.

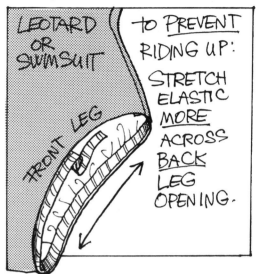

Fig. 3-12

• **For armholes, cut the elastic 1" less than the opening.**

• **For neckline openings, cut the elastic 1" less than the opening measurement.** Or, for deep back and front necklines, cut the elastic 3" less than the neck opening.

Application Tips

• When applying elastic to neckline and arm openings, **quartermark both the elastic and opening. Match quartermarks to apply evenly.**

• We prefer **the two-step topstitched casing method for applying elastic. It is sewn to the wrong side of the opening edge, then turned to the**

inside and topstitched from the right side. This application prevents the elastic from twisting and controls the distribution of ease. A two-step top-stitched elastic application can be done with the elastic ends seamed together to form a circle or with the elastic un-seamed.

• Whatever method you use, hold the elastic taut behind the presser foot, stretching it in front of the foot. Stretch only the elastic, being careful not to cut it.

To Apply Elastic in a Circle

(Fig. 3-13)

1. Cut the elastic according to the pattern instructions or ratio/measure-ment guidelines.

2. Overlap the cut ends 1/2" and zigzag to secure.

3. Pin the elastic to the wrong side of the garment opening, matching any markings.

4. **Adjust for 5mm serge-basting** (stitch density will increase when the

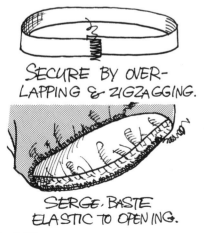

SECURE BY OVER-LAPPING & ZIGZAGGING.

SERGE-BASTE ELASTIC TO OPENING.

Fig. 3-13a

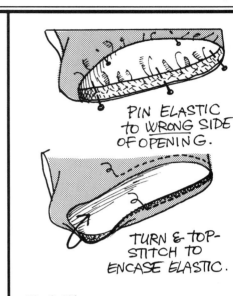

PIN ELASTIC to WRONG SIDE OF OPENING.

TURN & TOP-STITCH TO ENCASE ELASTIC.

Fig. 3-13b

elastic relaxes). Raise the serger presser foot and needle. **Place the elastic and garment (with elastic on top) under the presser foot** and next to the knives. Lower the presser foot and needle. Serge the elastic to the open-ing, overlapping the beginning of the serging. **Caution:** Remove any pins before they reach the knives.

5. **Turn the elastic to the wrong side, encasing the elastic.** Topstitch with your sewing machine to secure all layers (about 1/4" from the edge fold). See the topstitching options below.

To Apply Unseamed Elastic

(Fig. 3-14)

✎ **Note:** Some sergers have an elastic application foot for unseamed applica-tions; a screw on the top of the foot automatically adjusts the stretch of the elastic as it is applied. Considerable testing may be necessary to gauge the proper stretch adjustment. If you don't

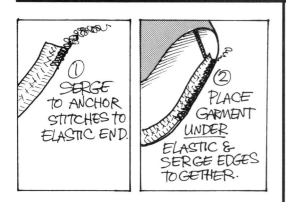

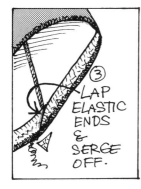

Fig. 3-14

have an elastic application foot, use this method with your standard serger foot:

1. Cut the elastic according to the pattern instructions or ratio/measurement guidelines.

2. **Serge several stitches in one end of the elastic to anchor the stitching.**

3. Place the **wrong** side of garment opening **under** the elastic and serge, stretching only the elastic and matching the markings.

4. **Lap the elastic ends 1/2" and serge, overlapping the previous stitching to secure.** Serge off.

5. **Turn the elastic to the wrong side, encasing the elastic.** Topstitch with

your sewing machine from the right side to secure all layers.

Topstitching Options for Encasing the Elastic

(Fig. 3-15)

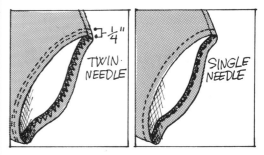

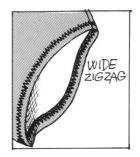

Fig. 3-15

• With a long, conventional straight-stitch (8 stitches/inch), topstitch from the right side. (When using 3/8"-wide elastic, stitch about 1/4" from the folded edge.) **Stretch the edge firmly while topstitching.**

• **With a twin needle and a conventional, long straight-stitch (8 stitches/inch), topstitch from the right side.** (The right side of this stitch has two rows of straight-stitching and the underside has one row of zigzagging, as shown.) Although this is a stretchier stitch, you still must stretch while stitching.

- **With a wide zigzag stitch, from the wrong side, stitch to secure, overlapping the serge-finished edge with the zigzag stitches.** Hold the fabric taut or stretch slightly while stitching.

- After stitching, hold a steam iron above the garment and **steam the elastic well** to return it to its original size.

Exposed Elastic Applications Using Gripper Bicycling Elastic

(Fig. 3-16)

1. Cut the elastic according to the pattern instructions or ratio/measurement guidelines—usually 1:1 or slightly less. (The rubberized side will

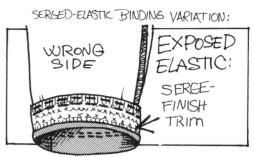

Fig. 3-16

be exposed and is the right side of the elastic.)

2. **Adjust for a long serger stitch length (5mm) and a medium to wide width** (3.5 to 5mm). (A longer stitch length places less thread in the seam, so the elastic will retain its elasticity.)

3. With right sides together and with a 1/4" seam allowance, sew the elastic into a circle with your sewing machine (Fig. 3-17a).

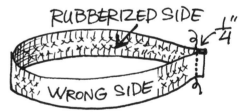

Fig. 3-17a

4. Pin the elastic to the opening, right sides together. Serge with the elastic on top (Fig. 3-17b). **Stretch the elastic to fit the garment opening, keeping edges even.** Hold the elastic taut in back of the needle and stretch it in front of the needle. Serge in short 1" to 2" increments, readjusting the elastic as necessary. (Be careful not to nick the elastic with the knife.)

5. **Fold the elastic to the wrong side and topstitch with your sewing ma-**

Stretch fashions can be easily hemmed and finished. A flounced edge, narrow rolled edge, narrow balanced edge, and a serged, turned, and topstitched edge are options outlined in Chapter 3.

A narrow
rolled edge
can be used to
serge-set
creases on knit
fabrics which
usually resist
holding a pressed
crease. Chapter 1
gives how-tos.

Sweaters can be serged quickly and professionally with minimum effort. To ensure matched seams at the bottom edge of ribbed cuffs or waists, stretch the ribbing taut. Stretch it the most at the end of the seam. More sweaterknit serging hints are included in Chapter 2.

Chapter 4 gives instructions for serging a simple, yet elegant lingerie nightshirt. The edges are serge-scalloped, using a rolled edge and the blindhem stitch on a sewing machine.

An elegant scarf is the quick-serged project discussed in Chapter 5. Edges are neatly and attractively finished with ThreadFuse™ melt adhesive thread.

Traced tulle is easy-to-make and very popular for veils, headpieces, accessories and accents in special-occasion serging. Chapter 6 gives details and variations.

Serging is the quickest and easiest way to sew faux fur. "Tails" are serge-seamed along the cut edge and turned before adorning this faux-tailed scarf. Project guidelines and special serging tips are in Chapter 10.

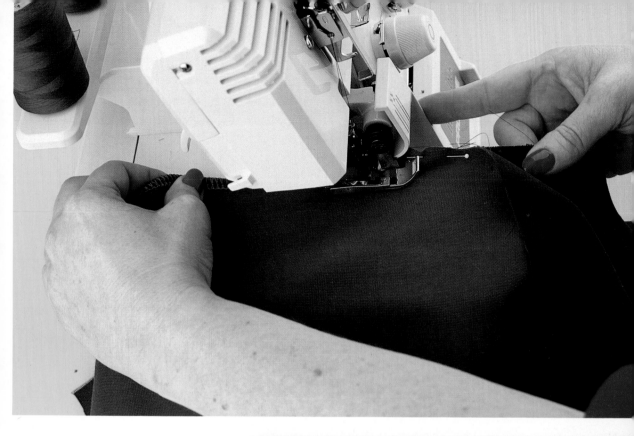

When serging velvet, hold the under layer taut in front of the foot to prevent slippage. Using pins inside the seam allowance also helps with seaming accuracy. More pointers on serging velvet and other pile fabrics are in Chapter 8.

A pretty portfolio is created by serging leather or suede. Crochet thread and buttons add an attractive accent and closure. Quick and easy instructions are in Chapter 9.

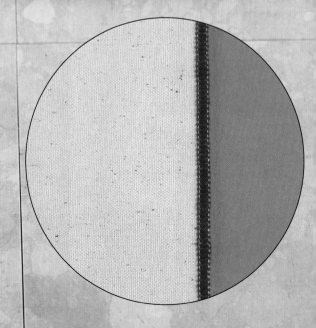

Bathroom clutter is neatly organized in this handy canvas catchall. A faux-braid finish adds a pleasing accent. See Chapter 7 for details.

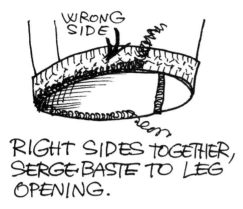

RIGHT SIDES TOGETHER, SERGE-BASTE TO LEG OPENING.

Fig. 3-17b

chine from the right side (Fig. 3-17c). Use twin needles or one of the other topstitching options for encasing elastic (page 51).

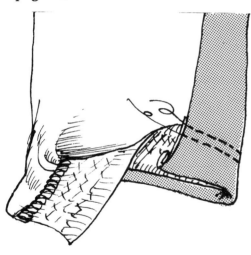

FOLD ELASTIC TO WRONG SIDE & TWIN-NEEDLE TOPSTITCH.

Fig. 3-17c

Finish the Lower Edge of a Bra or Camisole

(Fig. 3-18)

Encase 1-1/4" elastic in a fabric band and serge the band to the lower edge of the top. Here's how:

OVERLAP ELASTIC & ZIGZAG:

SERGE-SEAM LYCRA BAND:

WRONG SIDE

FOLD BAND OVER ELASTIC; QUARTERMARK:

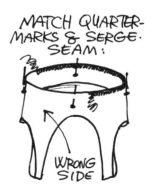

MATCH QUARTER-MARKS & SERGE SEAM:

WRONG SIDE

Fig. 3-18

1. Measure 1-1/4"-wide elastic around your ribcage and cut it to a comfortable length. Cut a matching or contrasting *Lycra*-blend knit strip 3-1/4" wide and 2" less than the measurement of the lower edge of the bra top.

2. **Sew both the elastic and knit strip into circles** (Fig. 3-18).

3. **Fold the knit circle, wrong sides together, over the elastic circle.** Quartermark.

4. Quartermark the bra. Matching markings, serge the band to the right side of the lower edge, stretching the band to fit the opening (Fig. 3-18).

Elasticized Binding

Elasticized binding stabilizes an edge and also serves as a decorative finish (Fig. 3-19). The binding can also extend into straps. Finishing is neat— on the inside of the garment or the underside of the strap.

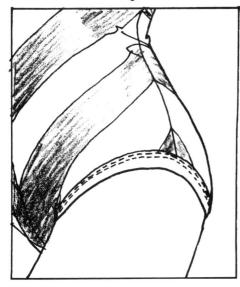

Fig. 3-19

1. **Cut the trim strip and elastic,** as shown (Fig. 3-20). (The greatest stretch should parallel the length of the strap.)

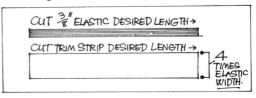

Fig. 3-20

2. Match the cut edges of the trim strip and the garment, right sides together (Fig. 3-21). With your sewing machine, **straight-stitch the strip to the garment using a 3/8" seam allowance.** Stretch both layers as you sew.

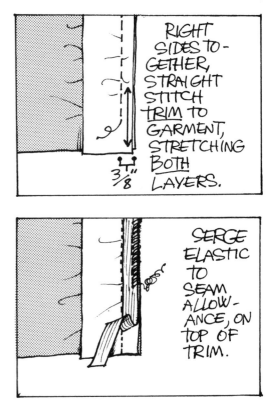

Fig. 3-21

3. Adjust the serger for medium-length and -width 3-thread stitching. **Serge the elastic to the seam allowance through all layers,** as shown (Fig. 3-21). Be careful not to cut the elastic.

4. **Fold the strip 3/8" to the wrong side,** matching the cut edge with the serged edges. **Fold 3/8" again,** encasing the elastic (Fig. 3-22).

5. With the right side up, use twin-needle topstitching to secure the binding layers (Fig. 3-22).

Fig. 3-22

6. For variation, serge-finish the long edge of the binding, trimming 1/8" (Fig. 3-23). Turn the serged edge to the wrong side and stitch-in-the-ditch to secure.

Fig. 3-23

Fast Hems and Finishes

• **Finish edges with a narrow balanced-stitch or narrow rolled-edge hemming.** Add flouncing (lettuce-leaf edge) by adjusting for a satin length and stretching the edge while serge-finishing (Fig. 3-24).

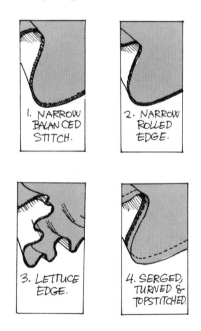

Fig. 3-24

☞ **Special Tip:** After serging, rigorously stretch the narrow hemmed edge for more pronounced flouncing. After laundering (which reduces the flouncing), stretch the edge again.

• **Serge, turn, and topstitch edges that need more weight but do not have the bulk or resiliency of elastic.** Serge-finish with a medium-width and -length balanced stitch. **Topstitch with your sewing machine with twin- or single-needle stitching, stretching as you sew.** Or secure with zigzagging (medium length and width).

Special Techniques

Serged Elastic Straps

For the quickest, neatest elastic straps, try this method. The elastic is sewn into the seam; it will never twist and the invisible stitching will never pop.

1. For two straps, **cut two strips of _Lycra_-blend knit and two lengths of elastic,** as shown (Fig. 3-25). (The greatest stretch should parallel the length of the strap.)

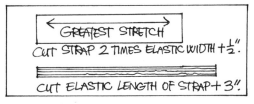

Fig. 3-25

2. Fold the fabric in half lengthwise, right sides together (Fig. 3-26). **Place the elastic on the folded fabric, aligning one side with the raw edges of the**

fabric strip. (Allow the extra 3" to extend beyond one end for turning later.)

3. Adjust the serger for a medium-length and -width, balanced tension 3- or 3/4-thread stitch. **Serge all the layers together—the elastic and fabric edges—without stretching.**

4. Using a safety pin, **thread the elastic through to turn the fabric tube** (Fig. 3-26). The seam will roll to the underside.

FOLD FABRIC, RIGHT SIDES TOGETHER, PLACE ELASTIC ON TOP & SERGE ALL LAYERS.

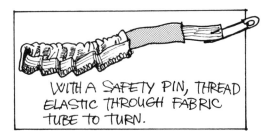

WITH A SAFETY PIN, THREAD ELASTIC THROUGH FABRIC TUBE TO TURN.

Fig. 3-26

5. Trim the elastic to the strap length and apply according to the pattern instructions.

6. Repeat for the other strap.

Altering Leg Height

In theory, a high-cut leg gives the illusion of longer and thinner thighs. In actuality, a high-cut leg opening can reveal too much, detracting from the longer-length illusion. For most of us, there's a leg-opening height that's a flattering compromise between creating a longer-legged look and covering figure flaws.

Some patterns give pattern cutting lines for both a low- and higher-cut leg. Others don't include different leg-opening heights, but alterations are easy if you follow these guidelines. The same adjustments can be made on patterns and on purchased swimsuits. (Obviously leg openings on ready-made swimsuits can be raised, but they cannot be lowered without adding bands, as shown in Figure 3-27.)

Fig. 3-27

• **To raise the leg cutting line:** (skip Step 1 if you are making the suit from scratch)

1. **Remove the leg elastic** and **rip out the side seams** to approximately 6" from the leg opening.

2. **Mark the side seams** 1" from the opening edges on both the front and back pieces. (The leg may be cut higher if desired, but it's wise to experiment 1" at a time.)

3. **Draw the new leg-opening line on both the front and back** (Fig. 3-28). Do not change the width of the crotch, and retain the curve of the back leg to prevent the suit from riding up.

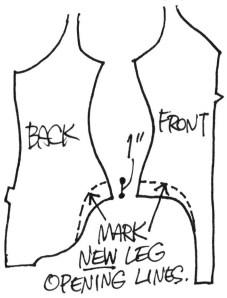

Fig. 3-28

4. **Try on the suit before applying the elastic to the leg.** Fine-tune adjustments as desired. **Remember,** the leg will be 1/2" higher when the edge is turned up and topstitched.

5. **Apply the elastic.** Because of the leg-opening alteration, the elastic ratio will necessarily change. (The higher the leg cut, the greater the elastic-to-fabric stretch ratio across the back leg.)

Measure the leg opening and cut the 3/8"-wide elastic 4" less than this measurement. Sew the elastic into a circle by overlapping the ends 1/2" and stitching securely. Pin the elastic to the leg opening. **The elastic should be 1" shorter than the front leg opening; stretch to fit the remainder across the back leg.** Turn the elastic to the wrong side and topstitch to encase it. For other elastic application tips, see pages 49 – 55.

• **To lower the leg cutting line of a pattern:** A similar process can be followed for lowering the leg-opening height on a pattern. Draw new leg-opening lines 1" lower at the side seams, tapering into the crotch (see Step 3, above). For this leg cut, the elastic is stretched less; measure the leg opening and cut the elastic 2" shorter. **Apply the elastic in a 1:1 ratio across the front leg opening, stretching to fit the remainder across the back leg.**

• **To lower the leg of an already-made suit:** Serge slenderizing bands (usually in a darker shade) to the leg openings.

1. **Remove the leg elastic and rip out the side seams** to approximately 6" from the leg opening.

2. Place tracing or wax paper over the suit, drawing a new line for the bands, as shown (Fig. 3-29). **Draw the bands 3" deep at the side seam,** tapering to the crotch seam. (The band portion extending beyond the suit will be the amount lowered.) Mark the upper band line on the pattern front and back; **add 1/2" seam allowances to all sides of the bands for the leg openings and seams** (Fig. 3-30).

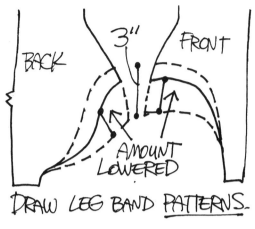

DRAW LEG BAND PATTERNS.

Fig. 3-29

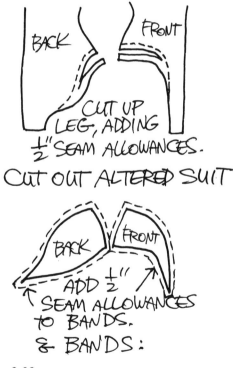

CUT UP LEG, ADDING 1/2" SEAM ALLOWANCES.

CUT OUT ALTERED SUIT

ADD 1/2" SEAM ALLOWANCES TO BANDS.

& BANDS:

Fig. 3-30

3. **Trim to the new leg-opening cutting lines, adding 1/2" seam allowances. Cut out the bands** and serge to the leg openings. (Seams should be

1/4" finished; trim 1/4" as you serge.) Serge the side seams, tapering into the original seamline.

4. Apply the elastic as described for lowering the leg opening (page 58).

Quick Tips

• **Use 3/8"-wide, rather than 1/4"-wide, elastic for most edge finishing.** The wider width provides more stability to the edge and will not weaken if accidentally nicked with the knife. If the pattern calls for 1/4" elastic, cut the pattern slightly larger at the elastic-encased openings.

• After serging and finishing with cotton elastic, **generously steam the elastic,** without touching the iron to the fabric. This will return the elastic to its original length.

• **Use the serged elastic strap technique** (page 56) for *Lycra* **belts,** using 3/4"-wide elastic and adding a fastener to the ends.

• For ease in tight-fitting woven pants, **add 2"-wide** *Lycra* **insets in the side seam,** serge-seaming the insets to the

Fig. 3-31

woven fabric (Fig. 3-31).

Project: Quick-and-Easy *Lycra* Tube

The *Lycra* tube is extremely versatile and can be worn as a belt, hip wrap, skirt, or bandeau by varying the depth

Fig. 3-32

of the tube (Fig. 3-32). Make one from nylon/ or cotton/*Lycra* fabrics.

• Tube sewing is not an exact science; **dimensions vary** with fit preferences and the stretchability of the fabric used.

• After cutting, fit (adjusting width and length) before serge-seaming and edge-finishing.

• Most tubes are constructed single-layer.

1. **Cut a rectangle** with the greatest stretch going the length of the rectangle, as shown (Fig. 3-33). Use these depths as a guideline:

Waist and hip tube	— 10" deep
Bandeau	— 15" deep
Skirt	— 20" deep

2. **Fit and serge-seam** the two short ends.

3. **Serge-finish** the two long edges, stretching as you serge.

4. Turn 1/4" to 3/8" to the wrong side and topstitch with a single or twin needle, stretching as you stitch (Fig. 3-33).

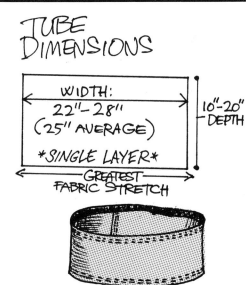

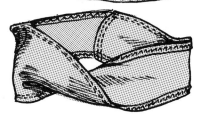

Fig. 3-33

4. Simply Serged Lingerie

Beautiful, feminine lingerie is perfect for gift-giving or adding to your own wardrobe. Applying exquisite laces, soft elastics, and delicate edgings to soft, lightweight fabrics allows you to create designs that rival the finest in ready-to-wear. Elegant lingerie is simply serged following quick and easy techniques—and you created it yourself.

Fabric Choices

The same lingerie fabrics used in ready-to-wear are now readily available at fabric stores and from mail-order sources (see Fabrics-by-Mail Directory, page 164).

Fabrics for lingerie don't have to be tricot. Many fabrics—both wovens and knits—are used in ready-to-wear. Whatever fabric you choose, it should be soft, lightweight enough to be worn under a garment, washable, durable, and wrinkle-resistant. Here are suggestions for suitable knits and wovens.

Knits

• **Nylon Tricot** is the most popular fabric for lingerie garments. It is strong, washable, and dries quickly. Tricot is wrinkle- and ravel-free, smooth, and drapeable.

Tricot is available in different yarn thicknesses, called denier. The higher the denier number, the heavier and more opaque the fabric. Forty denier is the most common, seen in panties, slips, teddies, and camisoles. Fifteen denier is sheer and lightweight, most often used as an overlay or for trims.

An advantage of tricot is its extra width—from 72" to 108". It stretches in the crosswise direction only. Tricot comes in an enticing assortment of colors, both pastel and bright; also look for prints and tone-on-tones.

• *Antron III* is a satinized nylon tricot that is nonclinging and antistatic. It is also available in a wide variety of colors. This fabric is slightly more expensive than regular nylon tricot.

• **Cotton Jersey** is a single-knit fabric that is lightweight and easy to sew. Cotton jersey is lovely to wear because of its softness and absorbency. It's also an antistatic fabric and, when blended with a synthetic, is wrinkle-resistant. Cotton jerseys are 54" to 60" wide and easy to find in dozens of colors, stripes, and prints.

Wovens

Woven fabrics are also popular for lingerie so they are included in this Knits section of the book. Because they're often cut on the bias, they have good stretch and drapeability, and are ravel-resistant. The width is usually 45" to 60".

• **Charmeuse** is a soft, drapeable, woven fabric of silk or polyester. Lightweight, it works particularly well when cut on the bias. Color selection is excellent.

• **Batiste** is a woven cotton or cotton-blend fabric noted for its light weight and delicate look. Comfortable in hot weather, it's also cling-free and easy to sew and launder. Batiste can be cut and sewn on the straight-of-grain or bias.

• Other wovens that can be used for lingerie are **soft satins, crepe de chines,** and **lace yardage** (both rigid and stretch).

If you cannot find lace fabric to match trim or fabric, create your own lace yardage. Do this by overlapping consecutive rows of lace trim and topstitching with the conventional zigzag stitch. Or serge them together with a rolled edge or narrow flatlock stitch

(Fig. 4-1). Repeat until the lace is the width you want. Then cut the pattern pieces from the newly created lace fabric.

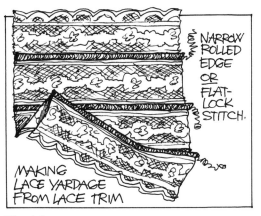

Fig. 4-1

Pattern Selection

All the major pattern companies offer lingerie patterns. Specialists like Stretch and Sew and Kwik Sew have several styles for both woven and knit fabrics and include serger instructions in their patterns.

If your pattern does not give yardage requirements for your selected fabric width, use the conversion guide shown here (Fig. 4-2). Use any fabric width and yardage requirement from the pattern envelope. Then find that width and yardage on the conversion guide. To convert to yardage of a different width fabric, follow the vertical yardage column for the width of your fabric. Yardage estimates do not allow for napped layout or matching designs. When using wide nylon tricot (104" to 108" wide), you will need just enough length for your longest pattern piece.

Lingerie Yardage Conversion Guide
(Fig. 4-2)

		YARDAGE											
	35"	1¾	2	2¼	2½	2⅞	3⅛	3⅜	3¾	4¼	4½	4¾	5
FABRIC WIDTH	45"	1⅜	1⅝	1¾	2⅛	2¼	2½	2¾	2⅞	3⅛	3⅜	3⅝	3⅞
	54"	1⅛	1⅜	1½	1¾	1⅞	2	2¼	2⅜	2⅝	2¾	2⅞	3⅛
	60"	1	1¼	1⅜	1⅝	1¾	1⅞	2	2¼	2⅜	2⅝	2¾	2⅞
	72"	⅞	1	1⅛	1¼	1⅜	1½	1⅝	1¾	2	2⅛	2¼	2¼
	108"	⅝	¾	¾	⅞	1	1	1⅛	1¼	1½	1½	1⅝	1¾

Fig. 4-2

Lingerie is simple in design with neither facings nor fastenings; the shaping is done with elastic. Select one versatile lingerie pattern and create a wardrobe of your own designs by shortening, lengthening, and embellishing the basic design (Fig. 4-3).

Fig. 4-3

Investigate ready-to-wear and mail-order catalogs for easy-to-copy ideas, like these:

• Lengthen a camisole into a slip or gown, allowing ample moving and walking ease, as shown (Fig. 4-4). You can also lengthen a T-shirt pattern into a nightshirt.

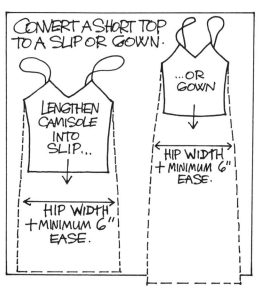

Fig. 4-4

• Wovens cut on the bias have knit-like stretch. Any pattern, including those designed for knits, can be adapted to a bias grainline. More fabric is required for bias-cut garments than is needed for those cut on the straight-of-grain. The serger is ideal for seaming because overlocking doesn't stretch the bias edges. Before cutting, change the straight-of-grain line on the pattern to a 45° angle. More fabric is required for ease, so add 1" seam allowances and fit as you sew (Fig. 4-5).

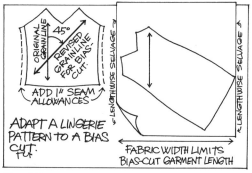

Fig. 4-5

The length of the finished bias-cut garment will be limited by the fabric width. Select wide fabrics for longer garments like slips. After cutting and before seaming, allow bias-cut fabric pieces to hang for 24 hours (pin the top of each piece to a hanger). This will eliminate stretching the garment after serging.

Timesaving Notions

 Note: For more notions information, refer to the general Timesaving Notions section in the Introduction and the Notions Guidelines for Specialty Fabrics chart on page x. Notions with fabric-specific explanations are explained here.

• **Scissors or a rotary cutter and mat**

• **Pattern weights**

• **Machine needles**

• **Pins**

• **Serger thread or lingerie thread**

• **Woolly stretch nylon thread**

• *ThreadFuse*

• **Transparent tape**—When topstitching lace to a garment, baste with small strips of movable transparent tape, such as Scotch Brand Magic Tape, placed at right angles to the lace. The tape can be sewn through and easily removed after stitching (Fig. 4-6).

• **Elastics** (see Elastic Tips, page 65)

• **Laces** (see Lace Tips, page 65)

Fig. 4-6

Elastic Tips

Elastics for lingerie can be found in most fabric stores. Many are dyed to match lingerie fabric. Standard widths are 1/8", 1/4", 3/8", 1/2", and 3/4".

Choose a good-quality elastic, one that is very stretchable and has complete recovery. For serging, it is also helpful to use elastic that will retain its width when stretched (Fig. 4-7). See Edge Finishing later in this chapter for how to measure and apply elastic.

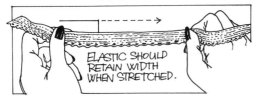

Fig. 4-7

Lingerie elastic is softer and stretchier than garment elastic, so it is more comfortable to wear. It's easy to recognize: one edge is usually decorative or scalloped, and the wrong side may be napped for increased comfort (Fig. 4-8).

A pretty accent for lingerie is **stretch lace elastic**. Made of *Lycra* (spandex) and nylon, it is available in 3/8" to 5" widths. The narrower widths make comfortable lingerie straps.

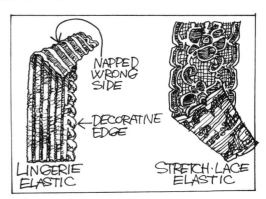

Fig. 4-8

Transparent elastic is an excellent choice for lingerie. Available in 1/8", 1/4", 3/8", 1/2", and 3/4" widths, it is lightweight, blends with any color, and is easily applied with the serger. After being stretched or sewn through, transparent elastic recovers to its original cut length.

Lace Tips

Lace adds femininity and elegance to your lingerie garments. It can be used as an edge finish, inset, or appliqué. Stretch lace can be substituted for lingerie elastic.

Laces are readily available in a variety of widths, fibers, and colors. Choose the best fiber and weight for your fabric. The choice of width is up to you. You'll find lace trim with two scalloped edges (**galloon**), two straight edges (**straight trim**), or one scalloped and one straight edge (**flounce**) (Fig. 4-9). A straight lace edge is easier to serge.

Laces come in colors that coordinate with or complement any lingerie fabric. For a popular ready-to-wear look, try using a contrasting color or a shade that is darker than your fabric. See

Edge Finishing later in this chapter for how to apply laces.

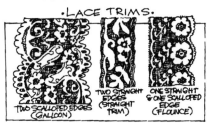

Fig. 4-9

Fabric Preparation

Pretreat your fabric with the same method you will use to wash, dry, and press your finished garment. Silk lingerie fabric may also be washed. (See silk care instructions, pages 81 – 82.) Don't forget to pretreat laces and trims to prevent shrinkage later.

Pattern Layout and Cutting

• When working with knits, lay out the pattern so the greatest stretch is in the crosswise direction.

• Determine the right side of **tricot** by stretching the fabric on the crosswise grain (which is also the direction of the greatest stretch) (Fig. 4-10). The fabric will roll to the right side. Mark the

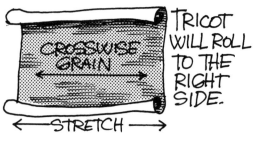

Fig. 4-10

right side with a washable marking pen or transparent tape.

• Most garments on the straight-of-grain can be cut double-layer, but always **cut bias-grain fabrics single-layer.** Lay out silky lingerie fabrics on a large, flat surface, making sure the fabric doesn't hang over the edge. Use pattern weights to eliminate pinning.

• Save scraps of fabric for testing, both on the lengthwise and crosswise grain. Leftover fabric also can be used for trim and for small gift items.

Pressing

Most lingerie fabrics require little or no pressing. **Caution:** If pressing nylon tricot, **use nothing hotter than a slightly warm iron** to prevent melting or scorching.

Seams and Seam Finishes

Lingerie looks, fits, and feels better when made with narrow seam allowances. The serger trims, stitches, and finishes a narrow seam in one quick step.

• **Narrow 3-thread balanced seam** (Fig. 4-11)—Adjust your serger for a **narrow stitch width.** Check your owner's manual to see how to adjust your serger. Use a **medium stitch length** (3mm).

• **Rolled-edge seam** (Fig. 4-11)— Adjust your serger for a rolled edge and a **short to medium stitch length** (2 to 3mm). This seam works well for sheer or lightweight fabrics. Using

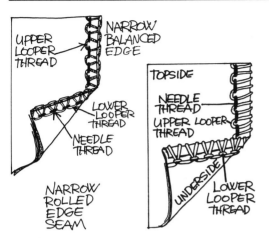

Fig. 4-11

woolly stretch nylon in the upper looper makes a soft, comfortable seam.

• **Narrow 3-thread flatlock seam** (Fig. 4-12)—Adjust the narrow, balanced stitch to a flatlock stitch by loosening the needle threads tension nearly all the way so that it is pulled to the edge of the fabric. Tighten the lower looper thread almost all the way so that it forms a straight line on the edge of the fabric. Adjusting the upper looper thread is usually not necessary.

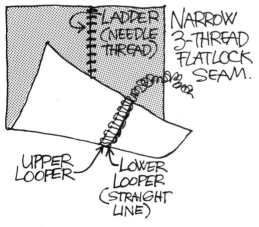

Fig. 4-12

For the least bulk on the outside of the garment, flatlock with right sides of the fabric together. Pull the seam flat—the ladder stitches will show on the right side. **Caution: Use this method only on knits or bias-cut wovens where the seams do not ravel.**

• **Narrow French serged seam** (Fig. 4-13)—With **wrong** sides of the fabric together, serge a narrow, balanced seam. Fold the right side of the fabric over the seam, aligning the seamline on the edge. With your sewing machine, straight-stitch close to the seam allowances, enclosing the seam. This method enhances the durability of woven fabric seams and gives a neat, professional look.

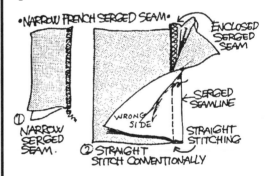

Fig. 4-13

Seaming Tips

Because the lingerie fabric is so soft, it can bunch under the presser foot when you start a seam. **To prevent bunching,** hold the thread chain taut behind the presser foot as you begin to serge; the serger will feed the fabric more evenly. **To prevent puckering,** always hold the fabric taut in front of and behind the presser foot when serging. Shortening the stitch length can also help. **Caution:** When taut-serging, do NOT pull the fabric through. This will bend the needle out of position and could cause needle and looper damage.

Edge Finishing

Elastic Edge Finishes

Because lingerie elastic is softer than all-purpose elastic and its stretch does vary, you may need to adjust the pattern's elastic measurement or guide.

• **The softer and stretchier the elastic, the shorter it should be cut.** Start by planning to cut the elastic 4" smaller than the waistline measurement. Mark the length on the elastic. Then simply pull the elastic around the waistline comfortably, add 1/2" for the seam, and cut to that measurement.

• **Using your serger, apply elastic to the right side of the fabric** (Fig. 4-14). **Use a medium stitch width (3.5 to 5mm) and the longest stitch length (4 to 5mm).** The longer stitch length prevents the elastic from permanently stretching out of shape.

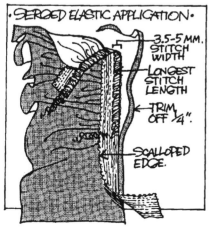

Fig. 4-14

Remember, place right sides together and hold both fabric and elastic taut behind the presser foot to eliminate bunched-up stitches. **Stretch only the elastic** in front of the foot. Be careful not to nick the elastic with the serger knife. And serge on the long straight edge of lingerie elastic, not on the scalloped edge.

• **When applying elastic by the flat construction method,** divide both the elastic and fabric into quarters and serge together in increments. To prevent bunching under the presser foot, serge a few stitches in the elastic only. Insert the lingerie fabric right-side up under the elastic and continue serging, trimming off the excess 1/4" of lingerie fabric, as shown (Fig. 4-15).

Fig. 4-15

• **An elastic application foot is available for some serger models.** It can be used only for the flat construction order, however, because the elastic is threaded through the slot on the foot. The elastic is stretched by turning a screw on the foot. The degree of stretch is determined by the tightness of the screw. Test before serging the garment—for more stretch, turn the screw to the right to tighten; for less stretch, turn the screw to the left to loosen.

• **When serging elastic in a circle,** overlap the ends 1/2" and zigzag them with your sewing machine. Divide the elastic and fabric into quarters and serge, following the basic application how-tos above.

• **The narrow flatlock stitch** (see page 67) is used in expensive ready-to-wear for applying elastic without adding bulk. Personal preference determines whether loop or ladder stitches appear on the right side of the garment. Serge with the wrong sides together for loops on the right side, or with right sides together for ladder stitches on the right side (Fig. 4-16).

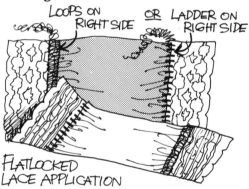

Fig. 4-16

☞ **Special Tip:** The flatlock stitch can be used to apply all elastics. However, to ravel-proof the edge of any woven fabric, serge-finish the fabric before flatlocking to the elastic.

• **A narrow- to medium-width balanced stitch** can be used to apply wide elastics of 1/2" or more. It creates a bulkier stitch than flatlocking but is also more durable and is seen frequently in ready-to-wear.

Laces Edge Finishes

Laces transform simple garments into elegant creations. Lace can be applied with several different techniques:

• **Balanced stitch application** (Fig. 4-17)—With the right sides together, serge the lace to the garment edge with a narrow balanced stitch. Lightly press the seam toward the garment. For variation, use *ThreadFuse* in the lower looper and serge with the lace on the top. Press and fuse the seam allowance to the garment.

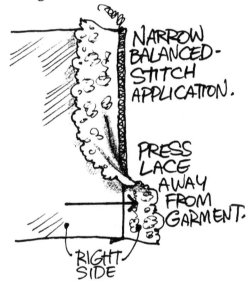

Fig. 4-17

• **Narrow flatlock lace application** (Fig. 4-18)—Use a narrow, medium-length flatlock stitch **when applying lace to a straight edge or as an insert.** Lace finishing is easiest with a straight-edge lace trim; for an insert, choose one with two straight edges. Serge-finish woven fabric edges before flatlocking.

Fig. 4-18

• **Rolled-edge lace application** (Fig. 4-19)—A rolled edge also can be used **if the lace is soft enough to roll easily.** For a decorative accent, place the **wrong** sides together so that the rolled edge will be on the right side of the garment.

Fig. 4-19

• **Mitered application** (Figs. 4-20 and 4-21)—**To apply lace to a shaped area that requires mitering** (as in a camisole top or the slit of a slip), it is easier to use a sewing-machine method. Overlap and topstitch with a narrow, medium-length zigzag on your sewing machine. Shape or miter the lace before applying:

Fig. 4-20

Fig. 4-21

1. Place the wrong side of the lace on the right side of the fabric with edges aligned.

2. Fold a pleat to the underside at each point, as shown in Figure 4-20, to miter and allow the lace to lie flat. Pin the pleats in place. Remove the lace from the fabric.

3. From the right side of the lace, zigzag the miter in place.

4. From the wrong side, trim the lace close to the zigzagging.

5. Place the mitered lace on the right side of the fabric and secure it with transparent tape. Zigzag along the lower edge of the lace.

6. From the wrong side of the fabric, carefully trim away the fabric seam allowance under the lace close to the zigzagging.

• *ThreadFuse* application (Fig. 4-22)— Serge-finish the edge of the garment. Using *ThreadFuse* in the lower looper and a wide, balanced stitch, serge the edge of the lace from the right side.

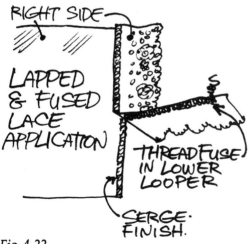

Fig. 4-22

Lap the wrong side of the lace over the right side of the garment. Fuse in place to secure.

Decoratively Serged Edge Finishes

Decoratively serged stitches finish edges quickly and easily.

• **Rolled edge**—Remember, tricot rolls to the right side, so always serge-finish the edge of the fabric with the right side down. Use fine decorative thread such as rayon or silk for a delicate, silky finish. Variegated thread used on a solid-color fabric adds subtle contrast. Try a shorter stitch length (1.5 to 2mm) for increased thread density.

☞ Special Tip: (Fig. 4-23): To create a scalloped finish, use the blindhem stitch on your sewing machine in tandem with the rolled edge. After rolling the straight edge, blindhem-stitch with your sewing machine, keeping the bulk of the fabric to the **right** of the needle. Allow the zigzag of the stitch to go slightly to the left of the rolled edge. Tighten the needle tension to make the edge more scalloped.

Fig. 4-23

• **Picot rolled edge** (Fig. 4-23)—Use a rolled-edge setting, but set the serger on a **longer** stitch length (4 to 5mm) and tighten the upper looper tension slightly.

• For **a more stabilized edge** on lightweight cotton jerseys or loosely constructed wovens, press 1/2" to the wrong side and serge over the fold with a rolled edge, being careful not to cut the fabric. Trim the fabric on the underside close to the stitching. **The rolled edge may be scalloped** with the machine blindhem stitch (Fig. 4-24).

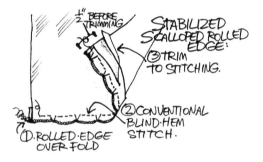

Fig. 4-24

• **Lettuce leaf (flounced) edge** (Fig. 4-25)—For fabrics with crosswise stretch (most knits and bias-cut wovens), set the serger for a rolled edge with a short stitch length (1mm). Serge the edge, leaving at least a 6" thread chain at the beginning and end of the serging. Stretch the edge, pulling with your fingers, after serging. The long

Fig. 4-25

thread chains prevent the thread from unraveling at the ends when the fabric is stretched.

• For a nonbulky finish at the bottom of a camisole, use a **narrow balanced stitch.** Or serge the edge, turn up a narrow 3/8" hem, and topstitch with a twin needle on your sewing machine.

Ruffled Edge Finish

Ruffles add femininity to the simplest of garments. Cut a ruffle the desired width by about 2 to 2-1/2 times the length of the edge where you will add the ruffle. Finish one long edge of the ruffle with a rolled edge or serged-on lace (see pages 71 – 72).

For easy serger gathering on lingerie fabrics (Fig. 4-26): If your serger has a differential feed, set it on 2.0 to gather the other long edge. For machines without a differential feed, tighten the needle tension almost all the way and use a long (5mm) stitch length to gather. Or serge over a heavy thread, secure one end, and pull up the other end to gather.

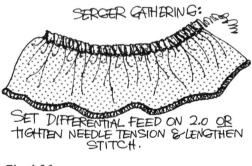

Fig. 4-26

Special Techniques

• **Altering ready-made lingerie is a snap with the serger** (Fig. 4-27)—To lengthen a lace-trimmed hem, cut off the existing lace and serge on wider lace. To shorten, cut off the lace, shorten the garment to the desired length, then serge the lace trim back on. (Or simply finish the cut edge in one step with a rolled-edge stitch.)

Fig. 4-27

• **Serged pintucks add a professional touch to lingerie** (Fig. 4-28)—Serge pintucks in the fabric before cutting out the garment. A rolled edge, scalloped rolled edge, or narrow balanced stitch (see pages 71 – 72) can all be used for pintucking. Serge rows of pintucks, using the presser-foot width as a spacing guide. (For wider-spaced pintucks, mark the stitching lines with a washable marking pen.) Try decorative rayon thread in the upper looper for a rolled edge, or in both loopers for a narrow balanced stitch.

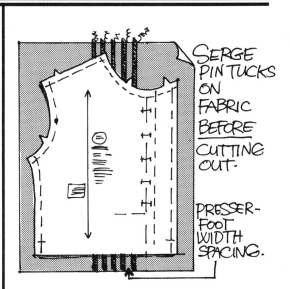

Fig. 4-28

• **Gather the top of a half-slip** with either of the easy methods described under Ruffled Edge Finish. Then simply overlap 1"-wide (or wider) elastic lace about 3/8" to 1/2" and topstitch with a twin needle on your sewing machine (Fig. 4-29).

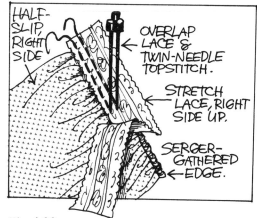

Fig. 4-29

• **Shir fabric with a 2-thread chainstitch** (Fig. 4-30)—To do serger-shirring, the movable knife and overedge

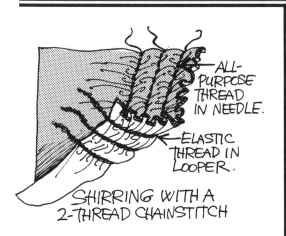

SHIRRING WITH A
2-THREAD CHAINSTITCH

Fig. 4-30

looper must be disengaged. This is not possible on some models, so check your manual.

Cut a fabric strip about two to three times the finished length desired by 3" to 6" wide; serge-finish one long edge before shirring. Or shirr the lingerie fabric before cutting it out (great for bodices of nightgowns). Use elastic thread in the looper and all-purpose or serger thread in the needle. The stitch length should be as long as possible. Tighten the upper looper tension in stages to increase the shirring effect. Serge the chainstitched rows about 3/8" to 1/2" apart, as shown (Fig. 4-30).

The shirred strip can be substituted for most ribbing applications: front edges and cuffs of robes and night-shirts, waistline edges of tap pants or slips.

• **Serge spaghetti straps for a slip or camisole** (Fig. 4-31)—Cut bias woven or crosswise knit fabric strips 1" wide by the strap length plus 1". Serge a

thread chain 6" longer than the strap. Center the chain on the right side of the strap fabric. Fold the fabric over the chain and serge the tube. Pull on the chain to turn the strap right side out.

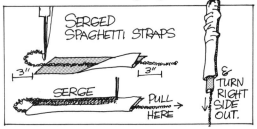

Fig. 4-31

Easiest Serging Order

(Fig. 4-32)

Using the **flat construction method** is the easiest way to finish the edges by serging or applying lace and elastic. Serge one seam, finish the edges, then serge the other seam. Be sure that the edges of the decorative stitching or the lace match at the second seamline.

☞ **Special Tips:**

• When sewing lightweight fabric with your sewing machine, put the needle into the fabric. Then, as you begin to sew, **hold on to the threads** to prevent the fabric from being pulled into the opening on the needleplate.

• If your fabric skips stitches:

— Pretreat the fabric before serging;

— Hold the fabric taut so it doesn't cling to the needle;

— Change to a smaller-sized, new needle; and/or

— Clean the residue of synthetic fabrics from the needle with rubbing alcohol.

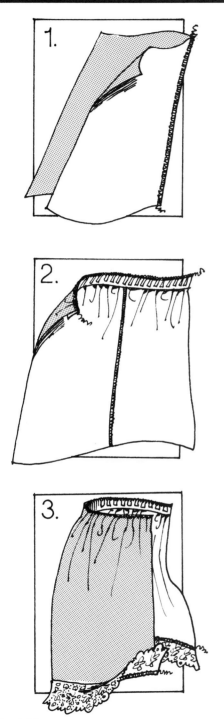

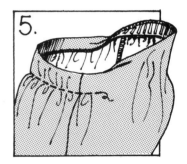

Fig. 4-32

Project: Quick-and-Easy Lingerie Garment

(Fig. 4-33)

Choose a simple, round-necked blouse pattern with a cut-on short sleeve. Lengthen the pattern to a nightshirt, allowing at least 6" of ease through the hips for comfort. Round the corners on the lower edge, shirttail-style (Fig. 4-34).

Fig. 4-32

For a designer look, choose a satiny tricot knit fabric or a silky charmeuse woven (cut on the bias).

☞ **Special Tip:** Pin the shoulder seams and make sure the garment will fit over your head. If it's too tight, trim out the front neckline 1/8" at a time until it slips easily over your head.

Fig. 4-33

How-tos

(Fig. 4-34):

1. Set your serger for a rolled edge. Serge the right shoulder seam.

2. Serge around the neckline. Scallop the edge by blindstitching with your sewing machine (see page 71).

3. Serge the other shoulder seam.

4. Finish the lower edge of the sleeves and the garment back and front with the same scalloped rolled edge used on the neckline.

5. Serge both side seams.

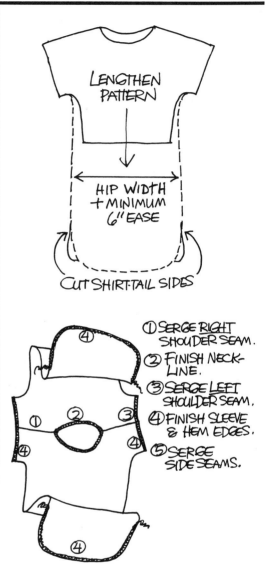

LENGTHEN PATTERN

HIP WIDTH + MINIMUM 6" EASE

CUT SHIRT-TAIL SIDES

① SERGE RIGHT SHOULDER SEAM.
② FINISH NECK-LINE.
③ SERGE LEFT SHOULDER SEAM.
④ FINISH SLEEVE & HEM EDGES.
⑤ SERGE SIDE SEAMS.

Fig. 4-34

5. Professional Results with Silky Fabrics

Silk and silk-like fabrics provide a classic, feminine addition to any wardrobe. Sewing these luxurious fabrics, however, has often been intimidating to even the most experienced seamsters. By following a few simple serging techniques, you can finish these garments easily and professionally.

Fabric Choices

A wide variety of silk and silk-like fabrics are available in most fabric stores and from mail-order sources (see Fabrics-by-Mail Directory at the end of the book). **Man-made fabrics, such as polyester and rayon, have so closely duplicated silk that it is difficult to distinguish the real from the synthetic.**

Silk

Silk is a natural fabric that is luxurious and comfortable to wear. Because of its absorbent quality, it keeps the wearer warm in winter and cool in summer. Silk is a strong, durable fabric, but it weakens when wet. Its resistance to wrinkling and pilling, plus its luster and drapeability, makes it an excellent choice for a garment to be worn for many years. Select a good-quality silk to save frustration in sewing. Good-quality silks have a tighter weave and generally are more expensive.

Rayon

This man-made, cellulose-fiber fabric resembles silk and its qualities but is more economical. It, too, is comfortable to wear, but it does not have silk's resistance to wrinkling. Rayon ravels more than silk, too. Rayon is not a strong fabric and loses 50% of its strength when wet.

Polyester

Polyester is a synthetic fabric that closely resembles silk in appearance but is less expensive. The fabric is very durable and drapeable, but its low absorbency does not allow it to breathe and makes it less comfortable to wear than silk or rayon. Blending polyester with rayon or a natural fiber, such as cotton and/or silk, gives it the absorbent qualities of the blended fiber.

Pattern Selection

Select a design that is soft and drapeable with few seams and darts. Ruffles, gathers, and shirring are good choices for these silky fabrics. Avoid tight-fitting styles and allow a minimum of 3" of ease at the bust and hip (Fig. 5-1).

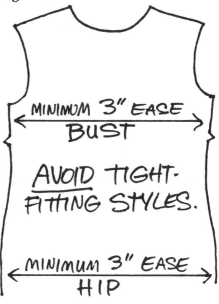

Fig. 5-1

Timesaving Notions

✎ **Note:** For more notions information, refer to the general Timesaving Notions section in the Introduction and the Notions Guidelines for Specialty Fabrics chart on page x. Notions with fabric-specific explanations are explained here.

• **Scissors or a rotary cutter and mat**—serrated scissors may eliminate fabric slippage when cutting.

• **Pattern weights**

• **Machine needles**

• **Pins**

• **Serger thread or lingerie thread**—Silk thread does not have to be used with silk fabric. Reserve this shiny, durable thread for top-stitching. It is expensive and difficult to find. One-hundred-percent cotton serger thread may be used on silk fabric. Because cotton thread is weaker than the silk fabric, when stress is applied the thread will break before the silk tears.

• **Rayon thread**

• *ThreadFuse*

• **Marking pen—Test water- or air-erasable pens on silky fabric scraps** before marking, even on the **wrong** side of the garment. Do not use water-soluble pens on dry-clean-only fabrics. Do not use either on silk.

Interfacing

Apply these simple guidelines to determine what kind of interfacing to use on silky fabrics.

• **The interfacing should be a lighter weight than the fabric** (Fig. 5-2). Feel the interfacing between the two layers of fashion fabric.

FEEL INTERFACING BETWEEN 2 LAYERS OF FASHION FABRIC.

Fig. 5-2

• **Pretreat fusible interfacing** by steam-shrinking it after cutting, just prior to fusing.

1. Press the fashion-fabric where the interfacing will be applied. Then position the interfacing, resin side down.

2. Hold the steam iron an inch above the interfacing and steam generously for a few seconds. Use the burst-of-steam feature on your iron, if you have it. You can often see the edges of the interfacing draw up slightly as you steam; the slight change in size due to shrinking does not affect the finished product.

• **Fusible knit is a quickly applied interfacing.** Make certain that the interfacing is properly fused and is not visible from the right side of the fabric. Tightly woven fabrics may resist complete fusion. **Do not trim the seam allowances from fusible interfacings.**

• **Test sheer, nonwoven interfacing, organdy, or crinoline, sew-in interfacing** (Fig. 5-2). Self-fabric is also a good choice, but make sure that the pattern does not show through the garment fabric.

Fabric Preparation

Pretreat your fabric with the same method you will use to wash, dry, and press your finished garment. Serge-finish the ends of the fabric to prevent raveling while pretreating (Fig. 5-3).

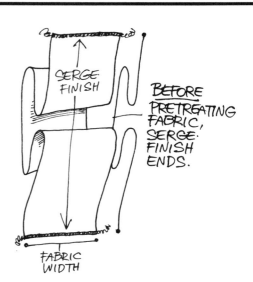

Fig. 5-3

Polyester fabrics can be machine washed and dried. Polyester will not shrink. It is important, however, to pretreat polyesters to remove any resin residues that could cause skipped stitches.

Check the care label on rayon fabric before pretreating. **If the rayon is washable, hand-wash it with a mild detergent and rinse well.** Most rayons will shrink, so allow a little extra yardage. Blot out excess water by rolling the wet fabric in a terry towel, then hang to dry. To speed drying, iron the fabric from the wrong side.

Silk fabric may be hand-washed. Silk will shrink, so purchase extra fabric to compensate. Prewashing eliminates water spotting and future shrinkage.

• Test a swatch of the fabric for texture change, colorfastness, and shrinkage.

• Swish the fabric in lukewarm water and a mild detergent in the sink or bathtub. Rinse thoroughly with cool water.

• Roll the fabric in a terry towel to remove excess moisture.

• Iron dry on a low temperature setting.

Pattern Layout and Cutting

When sewing with silks, fit the pattern and make all adjustments before **cutting out.** Ripping out seams and pinning can damage the fabric.

Slippery fabrics can be challenging to cut out. **A cardboard cutting mat can help control the sliding of the fabric** (Fig. 5-4). Stick long pins into the seam allowances and mat to prevent the fabric from sliding, or place the fabric on the flannel side of a vinyl tablecloth to hold it in place. Alternatively, **using a rotary cutter and pattern weights will also prevent the fabric from moving.**

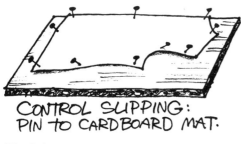

CONTROL SLIPPING: PIN TO CARDBOARD MAT.

Fig. 5-4

Pressing

• Avoid overpressing or overhandling silky fabrics. **Test press fabric scraps before pressing the actual garment.**

• **Press from the wrong side with a warm dry iron.** Steam can cause water spotting.

• **Press the serged seam allowances carefully so that the seam imprint will not show through to the right side.** Use a seam roll and strips of white bond paper between the seam allowances and the garment. Most of these fabrics need only light pressing.

Seams and Seam Finishes

• For the most professionally finished serged seam, **use a narrow seam allowance.**

• **For seams that will be pressed open** (Fig. 5-5), serge-finish the edges with a medium-length, narrow (2.5mm) and balanced 3-thread stitch. Straight-stitch the seam and press it open.

SERGE FINISH, STRAIGHT STITCH & PRESS OPEN.

Fig. 5-5

• **For seams pressed to the side** (Fig. 5-6), **straight-stitch the seam. Serge**

the seam allowances together close to the stitched seam, using a narrow, balanced 3-thread stitch, trimming about 1/4" as you serge. Lightly press the seam to one side.

STRAIGHT-
STITCHED
WITH
ALLOWANCES
SERGED
TOGETHER.

Fig. 5-6

• For lightweight silkies, **use a rolled-edge seam** (Fig. 5-7). Adjust the serger for a rolled edge and a short to medium stitch length (2 to 3mm). Serge the seam with right or wrong sides together, depending on the look you want.

NARROW ROLLED
EDGE SERGED
SEAM.

Fig. 5-7

• **To serge-seam,** adjust the serger for a medium-width (3mm), 3-thread balanced stitch with a 2mm stitch length (Fig. 5-8).

• Use a **serged French seam** to completely enclose the seam allowances (Fig. 5-9). With the **wrong** sides of the fabric together, serge a narrow, balanced seam. Fold the right sides of the fabric over the seam, aligning the

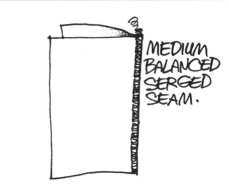

MEDIUM
BALANCED
SERGED
SEAM.

Fig. 5-8

seamline on the edge. Straight-stitch close to the seam allowances to enclose the seam.

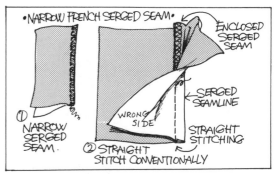

•NARROW FRENCH SERGED SEAM•
ENCLOSED SERGED SEAM
① NARROW SERGED SEAM.
SERGED SEAMLINE
WRONG SIDE
STRAIGHT STITCHING
② STRAIGHT STITCH CONVENTIONALLY

Fig. 5-9

Silky fabrics may pucker as they are serged or sewn and pressing will not remove the puckers. **For a professional, nonpuckered seam,** follow these guidelines:

1. **Shorten the stitch length** (2mm on the serger and 12 stitches per inch on your sewing machine).

2. **Adjust the differential feed to .8** to eliminate any puckering.

3. **Loosen the needle tension slightly.**

4. **Hold the fabric taut in front of and behind the presser foot.** Be careful not to pull the fabric through.

Edge Finishing

Eliminate facings when feasible (Fig. 5-10). Finished edges of silky fabrics should not be bulky.

Fig. 5-10

Serge-Finished Edge

Serge-finish the fabric edge with a narrow, balanced 3-thread stitch. **Turn**

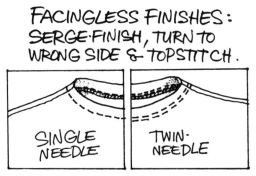

Fig. 5-11

3/8" to the wrong side and topstitch with a single or twin needle (Fig. 5-11).

Self-Fabric Binding

Finish the edge with self-fabric binding (Fig. 5-12). The cut edge of the garment will be the finished edge. If binding the neck edge, make sure the neckline will fit over the head after the binding is applied.

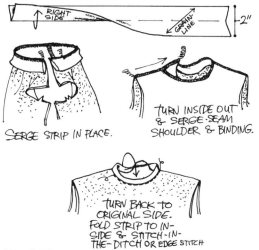

Fig. 5-12

1. **Cut a bias binding strip 2" wide by the length of the edge to be bound.**

2. Using one of the seaming techniques, serge-seam one shoulder.

3. Fold the binding strip in half lengthwise, wrong sides together. **Serge-seam the band to the opening with a wide, 3- or 3/4-thread balanced stitch.** When stitching the binding to a curved edge, such as a neckline, stretch the strip slightly around the curves. Pin the other seam together and check to make sure the opening will fit over the head.

4. Serge-seam the remaining shoulder seam through the binding.

5. Turn the binding to the wrong side, enclosing the seam, as shown (Fig. 5-12). **Stitch-in-the-ditch through all layers to secure.**

Ribbed Edge Finish

Apply ribbing to the edges of a silky garment. Convert a pattern or add the ribbing to a ready-to-wear garment. To add ribbing to the lower edge of a blouse, make sure the blouse has straight side seams (not flared or fitted).

1. **Mark and cut the blouse to the desired length.** Be sure to allow for at least 2" of blouson and 1/4" for a seam allowance.

2. For a 5" finished band, cut a strip of ribbing 10-1/2" wide and equal to the length of the waist or hip measurement, as shown (Fig. 5-13).

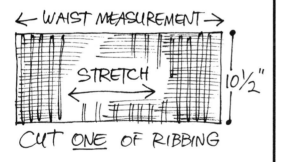

Fig. 5-13

3. **Straight-stitch the ends of the ribbing** (1/4" seam allowances), right sides together, and finger-press the seam open.

4. Fold the ribbing in half lengthwise, wrong sides together.

5. Pin together any overlap of the blouse front closure (Fig. 5-14).

Fig. 5-14

6. Quartermark the ribbing and the lower edge of the blouse with pins. Right sides together, **match the quartermarks, placing the ribbing seam at either side seam** (Fig. 5-14).

7. Stretch the ribbing to fit the blouse and serge it in place (with the ribbing on top) using a long, wide and balanced 3- or 3/4-thread stitch.

Fast Hems

Narrow hems work best with silky fabrics. Even hems found in the best ready-to-wear garments are serge-finished. Allow a skirt or dress to hang for 24 hours before hemming.

• **Narrow rolled hem** (Fig. 5-15)— Mark the hem, allowing 1/2" for the seam. Adjust the serger for a medium-length, narrow rolled edge. Serge-finish the edge, trimming 1/4".

Fig. 5-15

• **Serged, turned, and topstitched hem** (Fig. 5-16)—Trim the hem to 3/4". Serge-finish with a narrow- to medium-width, medium-length and balanced 3-thread stitch, trimming off 1/4". To ease the edge of flared hems,

use the differential feed at the 2.0 setting or ease-plus with forced hand-feeding. Turn up the hem and lightly press. Using the presser foot as a stitch-width guide, topstitch the hem in place from the right side.

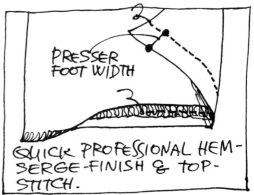

Fig. 5-16

For a variation, serge-finish the edge, then **turn up 1/4" and edge-stitch close to the fold.** Or press a 1/2" to 5/8" hem to the wrong side and **edge-stitch close to the folded edge and again 1/4" from the fold** (Fig. 5-17).

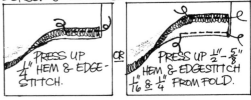

Fig. 5-17

• **Shirttail hems**— Serge-finish the edge with a narrow- to medium-width, medium- to long-length and balanced 3-thread stitch, tightening the needle tension to ease the curve. Press 1/4" to 3/8" toward the wrong side and top-stitch (Fig. 5-18).

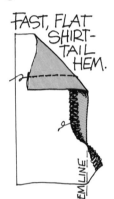

Fig. 5-18

Special Techniques

Serged Collars and Cuffs

Use the serger to serge collars and cuffs quickly (Fig. 5-19).

Fig. 5-19

1. Interface the collar and cuffs.

2. With the right sides together, **serge the collar to the under collar along the long outer edge,** as shown (Fig. 5-20).

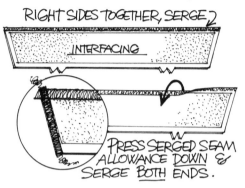

Fig. 5-20

3. **Press the seam allowance flat and then down** toward the undercollar. This forms a wrapped seam. After pressing, under-stitch with a conventional straight-stitch through all the seam layers (1/8" from the seamline on the undercollar side). This stitching will keep the seamline defined and flat.

4. **Serge the collar ends with the right sides together** (Fig. 5-20). (The seam serged in Step 2 should still be wrapped down toward the undercollar.) Press the seams flat. Turn the collar right side out and press again.

5. **Repeat these steps for the cuff,** pressing the seam allowance toward the cuff facing (Fig. 5-21).

To make an easy serged placket and apply the cuff, serge as shown (Figs. 5-22 and 5-23).

Easing the Sleeve

Polyester is difficult to ease, which presents a challenge for setting in a sleeve, especially one with a shaped

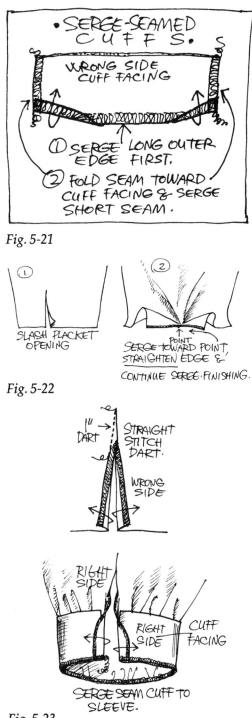

Fig. 5-21

Fig. 5-22

Fig. 5-23

cap. Use the serger when easing the sleeve. Mark notches on the sleeve cap with an erasable marking pen.

1. **Adjust the serger to a long, wide, and balanced 3-thread stitch.** Begin serging at the underarm seam and serge until you reach the first notch marking. At the notch, tighten the needle tension. Place the serge-eased stitches along the cut edge without trimming the fabric. Continue serging around the sleeve cap to the second notch (Fig. 5-24).

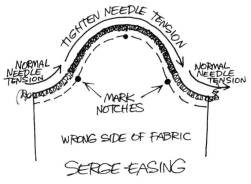

Fig. 5-24

2. Readjust the needle tension to its normal setting and finish serging. Pull the needle thread, if necessary, to ease the cap.

3. To set-in the sleeve, place one forefinger to either side of the presser foot. While sewing, pull the fabric horizontally to smooth the sleeve cap and prevent puckering.

Decorative Shirring

To create decorative shirring, use a 2-thread chainstitch and elastic thread (Fig. 5-25). Thread the chainstitch looper with fine elastic "knitting-in" thread. To shirr, you must be able to

Fig. 5-25

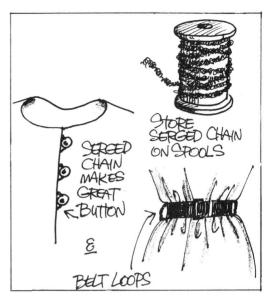

Fig. 5-26

disengage the loopers and raise the knife on your serger.

1. **Loosen the needle tension and then tighten incrementally for more gathering.** Lengthening the stitch will also increase the shirring.

2. **Serge the chainstitching rows about a presser foot's width apart.**

Buttonloops and Belt Carriers

When the serger is threaded with a new or different thread and adjusted to a rolled edge, **serge off a yard or more of serged chain.** Wrap the chain around an empty spool. Use these chains for making lightweight buttonloops and belt carriers (Fig. 5-26). Thread the chain through a large-eyed needle. Using the threaded needle, make a loop on the right side of the garment. Knot the chain ends together on the inside of the garment to secure.

Easiest Serging Order

Here are some guidelines for determining the easiest serging order with silky fabrics:

• **Serge in the flat construction order.**

• **Group similar tasks** such as rolled-edge serging, balanced serging, straight-stitching, and pressing. This eliminates threading and rethreading, as well as readjusting the serger.

• **Determine the type of seam to be used.** If the seam is to be finished and pressed open, complete the serge-finishing before straight-stitching any of the seams.

• **Serge continuously** (Fig. 5-27). Serge-finish and serge-seam continuously. Several edges can be serged without cutting the threads between each piece and without raising the presser foot.

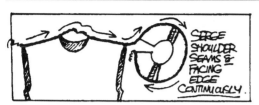

Fig. 5-27

- **Determine how the neckline will be finished.** It is easier to serge it flat rather than in a circle.

☞ **Special Tips:**

- When sewing lightweight fabrics with your sewing machine, put the needle into the fabric and **hold on to the threads when starting to sew.** This prevents the fabric from being pulled into the opening on the needleplate.

- If the machine skips stitches on silky fabric:

—Pretreat the fabric before serging;

—Change to a smaller size, new needle;

—Use rubbing alcohol to clean the needle from residue of synthetic fabrics; and/or

—Hold the fabric taut so that it doesn't cling to the needle.

- When making buttonholes in lightweight fabric, **place a piece of tissue paper or** *Tear-Away* **on the underside of the buttonhole** to prevent puckering while stitching. Tear it away after stitching.

- Before cutting a buttonhole, **apply seam sealant between the two rows of stitching to prevent fraying.** Apply the sealant carefully with a toothpick or pin. Allow it to dry; then cut the buttonhole open.

- If rolled-edge stitching tears away from the fabric edge, **lengthen the stitch and widen the bite** by moving the stationary knife to the right (Fig. 5-28). (Check your serger manual.)

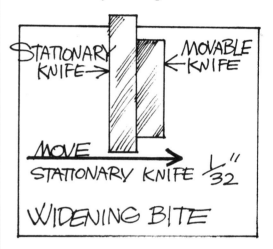

Fig. 5-28

- If rolled-edge serging doesn't turn the edge under, **use woolly stretch nylon or #80 monofilament nylon thread in the lower looper.**

- For easy serged sleeves, use the flat order of construction **with the garment side up.** The sleeve will automatically be eased in by the action of the feed dogs.

Fig. 5-29

Project: Quick-Serged Scarf

(Fig. 5-29)

For an over-the-shoulder scarf, a square 40" or larger is the most versatile. A 36" square is a common scarf size, but a larger scarf can be made from an all-over print fabric.

• When cutting out the scarf, **follow grainlines, if possible, without disturbing the print.**

• **Serge-finish the edges** of the silky scarf by using one of the following two methods. Use serger or all-purpose thread in the needle and loopers. (Try a decorative thread in the upper looper for more coverage and a designer look.)

Serge-a-Fold Finishing

(Fig. 5-30):

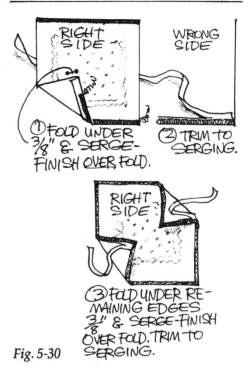

Fig. 5-30

1. Press under 3/8" to 1/2" on opposite edges, as shown.

2. Adjust for short, narrow rolled-edge hemming. For a picot edge, lengthen the stitch and tighten the upper looper slightly.

3. From the right side, serge along the two folds, being careful not to cut the fold.

4. With sharp embroidery or appliqué scissors, trim to the serging.

5. Repeat for the remaining sides.

☞ **Special Tip:** If the stitch does not roll over the edge when the lower looper is completely tightened down, try threading monofilament or woolly stretch nylon in the lower looper. These threads stretch as they feed through the serger and effectively tighten the lower looper beyond the capabilities of the tension adjustment.

Threadfused Finishing

(Fig. 5-31):

1. Thread the lower looper with *ThreadFuse* melt adhesive thread.

2. Adjust for short, narrow, balanced-edge hemming.

3. From the wrong side, serge-finish the edges.

4. Carefully press the serge-finished sides to the right side. (Try pressing from the middle of the edge and work out to the corners.) Only the stitch width should be turned to the right side. Another option is to serge and finish from the right side, then press and fuse to the wrong side.

5. Repeat Steps 2 to 4 for the remaining sides. Thread the ends back through the stitching.

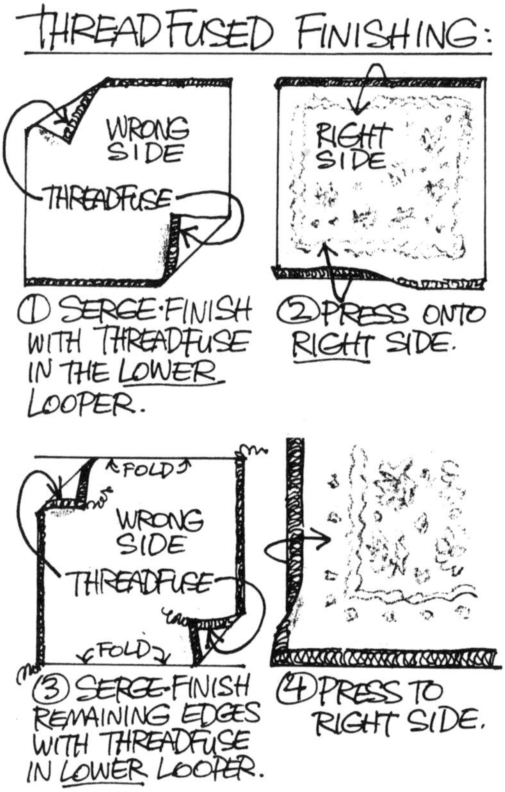

THREADFUSED FINISHING:

① SERGE·FINISH WITH THREADFUSE IN THE LOWER LOOPER.

② PRESS ONTO RIGHT SIDE.

③ SERGE·FINISH REMAINING EDGES WITH THREADFUSE IN LOWER LOOPER.

④ PRESS TO RIGHT SIDE.

Fig. 5-31

6. Mastering Special-Occasion Textiles

Handling special-occasion fabrics, such as satins, laces, tulles, and metallics, has been intimidating even to the most experienced seamsters. But now the serger has liberated us from the drudgery of yards of ruffles, edges, and seams. Serging provides fast, easy, and professional finishing. Details and accessories can be serged simply to rival the finest ready-to-wear.

Fabric Choices

A wide variety of fabrics can be used for special-occasion designs. Fabric choices are heavier satins and taffetas; sheer, lightweight tulles and chiffons; textured laces and sequins; and brilliant metallics. While some special precautions may be needed for each, serger techniques and uses are similar for all dressier fabrics.

When selecting fabrics and trims, look for better quality, even though your special garment may be worn very little or even only once. Choose tighter woven fabrics for less raveling when handling. Before buying, check for excessive wrinkling to avoid having to do a lot of pressing while sewing. If you are going to use trims on a garment, buy fabric and coordinating trim at the same time.

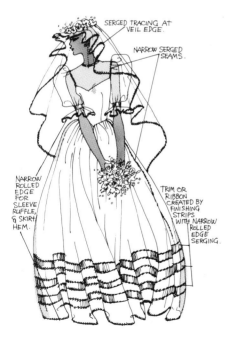

Fig. 6-1

Pattern Selection

Pattern companies offer a wide variety of patterns for special occasions. **Use your serger and the techniques in this chapter to add special creative touches to a basic design** (Fig. 6-1).

Sequinned and metallic fabrics are best used in patterns with a minimum of seams, darts, and closures. To eliminate seams, overlap pattern pieces, matching the seam allowances, before cutting (Fig. 6-2). Choose a flared design rather than one with pleats or gathers.

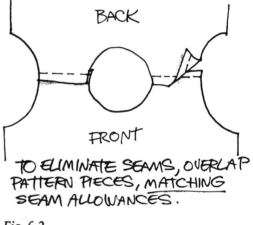

Fig. 6-2

Timesaving Notions

✎ **Note:** For more notions information, refer to the general Timesaving Notions section in the Introduction and the Notions Guidelines for Specialty Fabrics chart on page *x*. Notions with fabric-specific explanations are explained here.

• **Scissors or rotary cutter and mat—**

Except, don't use a rotary cutter on sequinned fabric.

- **Pattern weights**

- **Machine needles**

- **Pins**—Take care when pinning lace. Pins can easily become hidden in the fabric, so **place them parallel to the seamline to avoid damaging the knives** if you should miss one (Fig. 6-3).

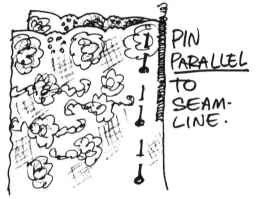

Fig. 6-3

- **Serger thread or lingerie thread**

- **#80 nylon monofilament**

- **Metallic thread**

- **Woolly stretch nylon thread**

- *ThreadFuse*

- **Marking pen**—**Test air-soluble pens on fabric scraps** before marking even the wrong side of the garment.

- **Glue**—Use a **fabric glue stick for quick basting** when underlining. It gives a fast-drying temporary bond. Use permanent fabric glue that dries clear as a quick way of attaching pearls and beads to fabric.

- **Masking tape**—**Use masking tape when cutting and finishing seams of sequinned fabric.** See pages 96 – 97.

Interfacing

Choosing the right interfacing for special-occasion fabrics can be tricky. Most silks, silkies, satins, and laces are tightly woven, smooth-surfaced, **or sheer, so fusible interfacings are risky.**

Copy the Pros with Crinoline Interfacing

Crinoline, **a 100% nylon netting, is the perfect interfacing choice** because of its reasonable price (usually about $2.30/yard), wide width (52" to 54"), nondirectional grain, and suitability to most special fabrics (Fig. 6-4). Sheer netting blends with any color and doesn't alter the look or hand of laces or sheers. The crispness adds body to areas such as collars and bows. Keep several yards on hand for interfacing, sleeve headers, or ruffled tiers on underslips.

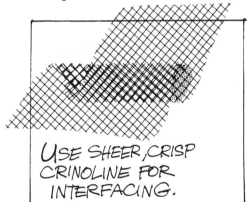

Fig. 6-4

Lining

Metallic and sequinned fabric should be completely lined to the edge of the garment to prevent irritation when worn next to the skin. Another option is to bind the edges with a softer fabric.

Fabric Preparation

Pretreat your fabric with the same method you will use to wash, dry, and press the finished garment. Metallics and sequinned fabrics do not shrink and usually do not need to be pretreated. Sequinned fabric should be cleaned by a dry cleaner without heat and pressing.

Pattern Layout and Cutting

If you need several dresses for a group, **cut out all the gowns at one time.** You'll economize on fabric, plus ensure uniformity of grain direction.

All special-occasion fabrics should follow the "with nap" pattern layout for uniform color shading and metallic sheen. When laying out, use pattern weights instead of pins to prevent snagging and marring the fabric.

When cutting sequinned fabric, follow these guidelines:

• **Cut the fabric with the sequins running down the garment.** The fabric should feel smooth as you rub your hand from the neckline to the lower edge.

• Cut the fabric single-layer with the sequinned side up.

• Tape the pattern to the fabric around the edges with masking tape (Fig. 6-5).

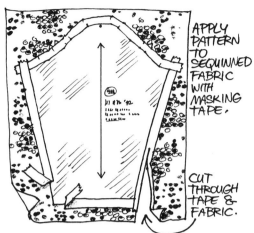

APPLY PATTERN TO SEQUINNED FABRIC WITH MASKING TAPE.

CUT THROUGH TAPE & FABRIC.

Fig. 6-5

Cutting through the masking tape and fabric prevents the cut sequins from scattering. Leave the remaining masking tape on the fabric to keep the sequins from raveling at the cut edges.

Pressing

• **Test-press fabric scraps before pressing the actual garment.** Most special-occasion fabrics need a light pressing.

• **Press from the wrong side with a warm, dry iron.** Steam can waterspot satins and taffetas.

• **Press the serged seam allowances carefully so that the seam imprint does not show through to the right side.** Use a seam roll and strips of white bond paper between the seam allowances and the garment.

• Metallics and sequinned fabrics are heat- and moisture-sensitive. Steam may permanently tarnish or dull the surface. **Finger-press the seams or press with a dry iron from the wrong side, using a press cloth.**

Seams and Seam Finishes

Test seam and seam finishes on scraps of the garment fabric (Fig. 6-6). Before stitching any seams in sequinned fabrics, remove the masking tape and all sequins from the seam allowances. Serging over even one pesky sequin will break a needle every time. Instead of snipping the joining threads, snip the sequins (Fig. 6-7). Threads remain intact to hold the other sequins securely. Simply cut a pie-shaped wedge from each sequin—from the outer edge to the center hole—and use serger tweezers to slip the sequin out of its holding stitch.

Fig. 6-7

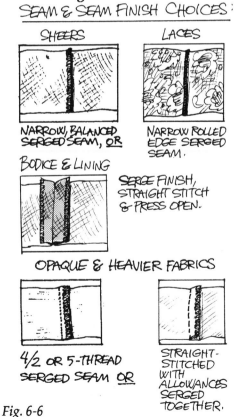

SEAM & SEAM FINISH CHOICES:

SHEERS — NARROW, BALANCED SERGED SEAM, OR

LACES — NARROW ROLLED EDGE SERGED SEAM.

BODICE & LINING — SERGE FINISH, STRAIGHT STITCH & PRESS OPEN.

OPAQUE & HEAVIER FABRICS

4/2 OR 5-THREAD SERGED SEAM OR

STRAIGHT-STITCHED WITH ALLOWANCES SERGED TOGETHER.

Fig. 6-6

• **Serge inconspicuous seams.** Sheers and laces can be seamed discreetly with a narrow rolled edge; test the stitch length and thread types on garment scraps for maximum durability without sacrificing softness.

• **For the bodice and bodice lining, opt for conventional straight-stitched and pressed-open seams.** (Finishing the bodice seam allowances is unnecessary unless the fabric is sheer; then finish after fitting.)

• **Press the seams lightly, or simply finger-press.** To prevent making a seam-edge imprint on the right side of the garment, place a strip of white bond paper under the seam edge(s).

• **Serge and sew all long skirt seams in the same direction** so that the garment will hang smoothly and evenly.

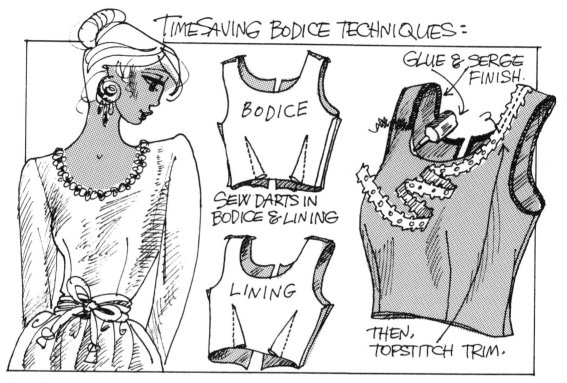

Fig. 6-8

Special Techniques

Timesaving Bodice Technique

Eliminate facings. Instead, line to the bodice edge (Fig. 6-8). Dart and seam the bodice and lining separately. Then place them wrong sides together and join at the neckline, armholes, and center-back seams. If underlining, treat the bodice and underlining as one layer.

1. **Sew the bodice and lining darts.**

2. Wrong sides together, **glue the lining to the bodice.** (Dab glue on the seam allowances.)

3. **Serge the bodice and lining together** along the neckline and center-back seam edges.

4. With the wrong side of the lace trim to the right side of the neckline, **topstitch in place, covering the serging** (Fig. 6-8).

Serging Sheer Yokes

Sheer or lace yoke applications can be tricky, but they're nearly mistake-proof if you follow these sewing and serging steps. This technique allows the bodice and yoke to fit flush with the body, without excess bulk (Fig. 6-9).

1. **Serge the bodice and lining** wrong sides **together.**

2. **Lap the sheer yoke 1/2" under the bodice** and edge-stitch.

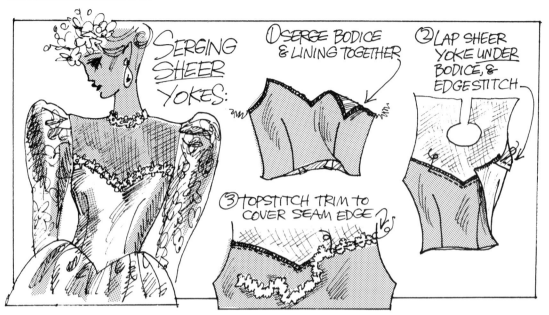

Fig. 6-9

3. **Topstitch the lace trim over the edge,** covering the serging.

4. **Serge-finish the yoke neckline edge** and topstitch lace trim over the edge. Or sew on a collar.

Quick Lace Collar

For a lovely high neckline, apply this collar quickly, using lace trim with at least one decoratively shaped or finished edge (Fig. 6-10).

1. **Cut out the lace trim and the crinoline facing,** as shown.

2. **Serge to finish and soften the crinoline facing edges.** (Woolly stretch nylon works well in the loopers.)

3. **Topstitch the collar to the crinoline facing,** wrong sides together.

4. Right sides together, **serge the collar to the neckline edge.**

5. Lightly **press the seam toward the collar and topstitch** to secure.

Variation: If both lace edges are shaped or finished, serge-finish the crinoline facing and serge- seam to the neckline. Then edge-stitch the collar over the facing.

Sleeve Techniques

• **Straight-stitch the sleeves to the bodice;** serge-finish the allowances together, close to the straight-stitching.

• **Reinforce the sleeve caps with crinoline headers.** Cut out, fold, and round as shown (Fig. 6-11). Gather along the curved edge to about 6". After gathering, serge the edges to-

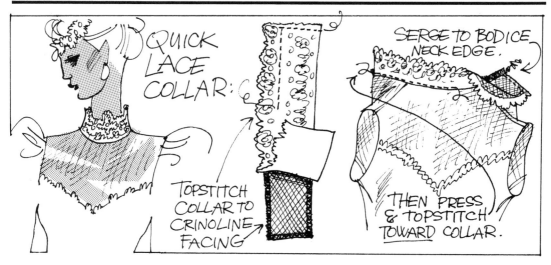

QUICK LACE COLLAR:

TOPSTITCH COLLAR TO CRINOLINE FACING

SERGE TO BODICE NECK EDGE.

THEN PRESS & TOPSTITCH TOWARD COLLAR.

Fig. 6-10

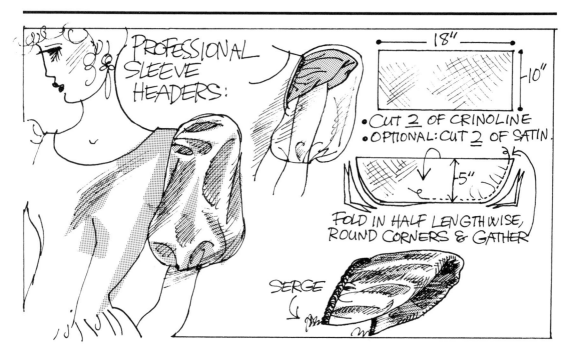

PROFESSIONAL SLEEVE HEADERS:

18"

10"

• CUT 2 OF CRINOLINE
• OPTIONAL: CUT 2 OF SATIN.

5"

FOLD IN HALF LENGTHWISE, ROUND CORNERS & GATHER

SERGE

Fig. 6-11

Fig. 6-12

gether. Fit and then straight-stitch into the top of the sleeve seam; the crinoline won't show through laces and sheers. Cover the header with satin if the scratchiness of the crinoline is irritating.

• **Finish shaped sleeve hems with lace trim.** Serge-finish the edge, then lap and topstitch the lace trim (Fig. 6-12).

Easiest Elastic Casing

(Fig. 6-13)

1. **Mark the lengths needed** on a long strip of elastic, but do not cut.

2. **Serge-finish the hem edge** of the sleeve.

3. **Press the casing to the wrong side. Insert the elastic,** securing one end with straight-stitching.

4. **Straight-stitch the casing,** pulling the elastic to the marking. Secure the end of the elastic with straight-stitching. Cut the elastic.

Variation: To attach lace trim or a ruffle to the casing, lap the serge-finished edge of lace under the casing

Fig. 6-13

and topstitch before inserting and pulling up the elastic (Fig. 6-14).

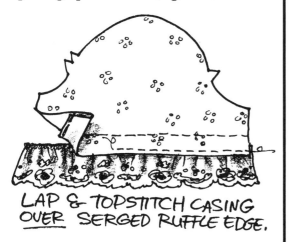

LAP & TOPSTITCH CASING OVER SERGED RUFFLE EDGE.

Fig. 6-14

Serge the sleeve seam, catching the elastic in the stitching.

Fast Hems

• Allow full or flared skirts to hang **for at least 24 hours** before marking and serging the hem.

• On lightweight and sheer fabrics, **serge-finish the hem edge.** A narrow rolled-edge stitch is recommended.

• On medium-weight and heavy fabrics, **serge-finish, turn, and top-**

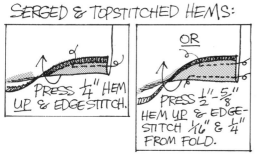

SERGED & TOPSTITCHED HEMS:

PRESS 1/4" HEM UP & EDGESTITCH.

OR

PRESS 1/2"-5/8" HEM UP & EDGESTITCH 1/16" & 1/4" FROM FOLD.

Fig. 6-15

stitch hems, as shown (Fig. 6-15). Use the wider hem when the garment requires some hem weight to control billowing.

• **Try horsehair-type braid on full-length flared hems** that must stand away from the wearer for unencumbered walking. This is actually stiffened nylon flat braid, available in several widths. The 1/2" width is the most versatile. Serge-finish the hem, lap the braid 3/8" over the right side of the hem, and edge-stitch (Fig. 6-16). Press up (aligning the seam at the fold) and, from the right side, stitch-in-the-ditch of the side seams to secure. This is all you need to hold up the hem.

HORSE-HAIR BRAID HEM:

FOLD LINE

SERGE-FINISH HEM, LAP BRAID 3/8" & EDGESTITCH.

PRESS TO WRONG SIDE & STITCH-IN-THE-DITCH AT SIDE SEAMS.

Fig. 6-16

• **For decorative finishing** (Fig. 6-17), serge-finish with a narrow rolled edge,

SCALLOPED LACE HEM:

EDGE FINISH WITH NARROW ROLLED HEM. THEN, LAP LACE & TOPSTITCH.

Fig. 6-17

then lap and topstitch the lace trim, covering the serging. Use a lace galloon (two scalloped edges) or flounce (one scalloped edge) trim for a scalloped hem.

Special Occasion Finishes

Serged Ruffles

Now, with the help of your serger, you can make several yards of ruffles in one short sewing session (Fig. 6-18). For speed and accuracy, cut out ruffles with a rotary cutter on a large cutting mat. Bias ruffles gather and drape beautifully, but they demand more yardage than those made crosswise or lengthwise.

Fig. 6-18

• **To make a serged double ruffle** (Fig. 6-19), cut the length two to three times the edge measurement and the

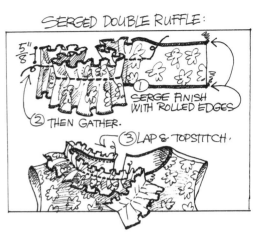

Fig. 6-19

desired width. Serge-finish both long edges of the ruffle with a narrow rolled edge. Gather the ruffle 5/8" from one finished edge.

• **For a serged-lace edge trim** (Fig. 6-20), overlap rows of serging, using a balanced tension, widest-width, and longest-length 3/4-thread stitch. For a delicate look well suited to sheers and laces, use lightweight serger thread in the loopers and #80 monofilament nylon thread in the needle. Metallic or rayon threads also can be used in the loopers.

1. **Start by serge-finishing the edge.**

2. **Overlap the next row,** positioning the needle inside the loops of the previous row, allowing all but the needle thread to hang over the edge. Leave a 6" tail at the beginning and end of the rows.

3. **For a wider trim,** continue adding rows.

4. **To create a ruffled effect,** pull and stretch the lace edge.

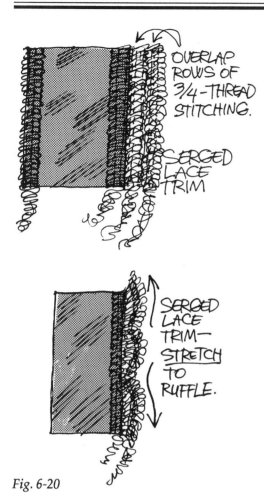

OVERLAP ROWS OF 3/4-THREAD STITCHING.

SERGED LACE TRIM

SERGED LACE TRIM— STRETCH TO RUFFLE.

Fig. 6-20

FISHLINE RUFFLES:

Fig. 6-21

Test this technique on garment scraps. Soft, lightweight, and bias-grain fabrics will flounce more readily than crisper, heavier, and straight-grain fabrics. (Grain isn't a consideration when using tulle because it has no grain.) If the finished edge is ravelly or pulls off easily, cut ruffle strips on the lengthwise grain.

1. **Adjust for medium-length, narrow rolled-edge hemming.** Use serger, rayon, or woolly stretch nylon thread for the upper looper and serger or #80 monofilament nylon thread for the lower looper and needle.

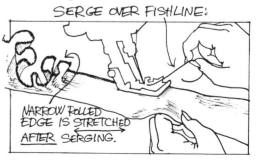

SERGE OVER FISHLINE:

NARROW ROLLED EDGE IS STRETCHED AFTER SERGING.

Fig. 6-22

• **For extra body and more flare along ruffled edges, serge over fishline** (Fig. 6-21). You'll find it at most drug, discount, and sporting goods stores. It comes in blue and clear colors. Use 15- to 17-pound fishline for lighter weights like tulle; 25-pound for heavier fabrics like taffeta. For any fabric color other than a matching blue, use clear fishline. (Even when serged with a short stitch length, blue fishline peeks through.) A 650-yard spool costs about $6 and will finish yards and yards of ruffles.

2. **Feed the fishline strand over the front and under the back of the foot,** between the needle and the cutting line; leave long fishline tails at both ends of the edge (Fig. 6-22).

☞ **Special Tip: For hands-free fishline application, thread the fishline through a cording-foot hole or slot.** (Cording feet are now available as standard or optional accessories for most serger models and brands.) The hole or slot in the foot **will guide the fishline directly between the needle and the knife,** centering it under the upper looper stitching and to the left of the cutting assembly.

3. **Serge over the fishline for 2" to 3", then slip the fabric underneath.** Steer with the fishline between the needle and the knife, being careful not to cut it (Fig. 6-22).

4. **Stretch after serging** to increase the flouncing.

Serge to Gather Trim

1. **Buy trim two** (for medium-weight) **to three** (for lightweight and sheer) times the finished length on the garment.

2. **Gather one edge,** using a medium stitch width and the differential feed (2.0 setting) or the longest stitch length and tightened needle tension. With your left index finger, **hold the fabric layers behind the presser foot to increase the gathering action.** If you want even more gathers, pull the needle thread(s). Or for heavier fabrics, serge over topstitching thread, secure one end, and pull the other to gather.

Variation: Gather both sides of the trim, lace, or a self-fabric strip, using the methods described above (Step 2). Serge the strip between seam edges as a decorative insert. This insert, called "puffing," is popular as an element of heirloom serging, a speedy simulation of French handsewing. Or discreetly enlarge a gown one or two sizes by inserting puffing in the seams (Fig. 6-23).

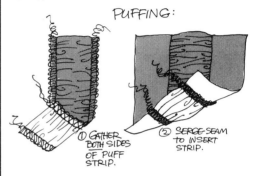

PUFFING:

① GATHER BOTH SIDES OF PUFF STRIP.

② SERGE SEAM TO INSERT STRIP.

Fig. 6-23

Sashes and Cummerbunds

Serging eliminates the time-consuming turning step usually required when making sashes or cummerbunds. Single-layer sashes or cummerbunds are preferred because they aren't bulky and never slip out of position.

1. **Cut out** the fabric on the bias, as shown (Fig. 6-24).

2. **Serge-finish all four edges.** Carefully press 5/8" to the wrong side of all four edges.

3. Try on the garment and **mark the side seams on the sash.**

4. **Gather or softly pleat the sash** to a 2" depth at the side seam markings.

5. Place the wrong side of the sash to the right side of the garment (at the

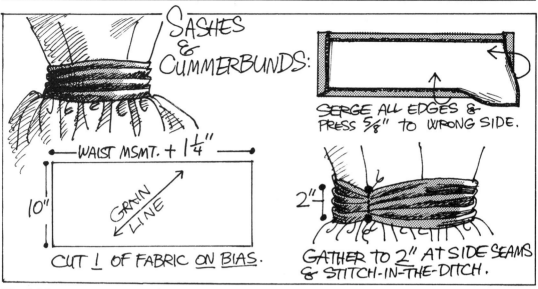

Fig. 6-24

waistline). **Stitch-in-the-ditch at the side seams,** over the gathering stitching.

6. **Topstitch** at the center back opening. Finish with a matching bow at the center back (see Fig. 6-25).

Beautiful Bows

Bows will always be popular accents for bridal and formal wear (Fig. 6-25). **Interfacing with crinoline helps maintain the bow's shape.**

1. **Cut out** the fabric and crinoline, as shown (Fig. 6-26).

2. **Serge-finish** the edges of the bow.

3. **Center the crinoline** on the wrong side of the bow. On each long side of the bow, press 2" to the wrong side, over the crinoline.

4. **Serge-finish** the bow ends.

Fig. 6-25

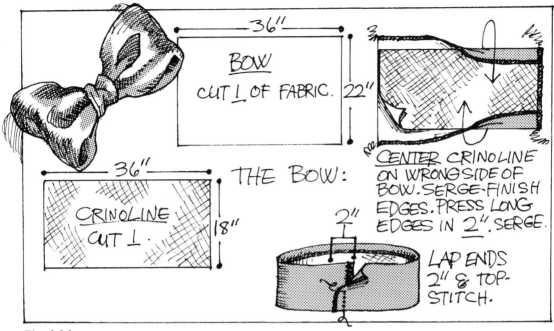

THE BOW:

36" — BOW CUT 1 OF FABRIC. 22"

36" — CRINOLINE CUT 1. 18"

CENTER CRINOLINE ON WRONG SIDE OF BOW. SERGE-FINISH EDGES. PRESS LONG EDGES IN 2". SERGE.

2"

LAP ENDS 2" & TOP-STITCH.

Fig. 6-26

5. **Lap the ends 2",** forming a circle, and topstitch to secure.

6. **Cut out the tie,** as shown (Fig. 6-27).

7. **Fold the tie** in half lengthwise,

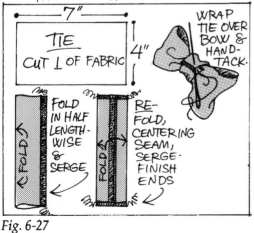

THE TIE FOR BOW:

7" — TIE CUT 1 OF FABRIC 4"

FOLD IN HALF LENGTHWISE & SERGE

RE-FOLD, CENTERING SEAM, SERGE-FINISH ENDS

WRAP TIE OVER BOW & HAND-TACK.

Fig. 6-27

wrong sides together, and **serge-seam.**

8. **Refold,** centering the seam. Serge-finish the ends.

9. **Wrap the tie around the bow,** as shown. Hand-tack.

10. **Handsew** *Velcro* **squares** on the bow and the garment to fasten in position.

   Variation: For a double bow, cut out two 22" by 24" rectangles, as shown (Fig. 6-28). **Straight-stitch** right sides together, leaving a 2" opening for turning. Trim the corner seam allowances and turn right side out. Press carefully. Center the smaller bow (described above) over the larger bow, wrapping and sewing the tie around all thicknesses.

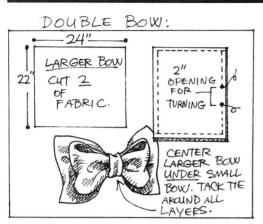

Fig. 6-28

Beaded Trim

Strands of pearls, beads, or sequins can highlight a seam or edge, adding custom elegance to gowns, headpieces, and accessories. **Create trim or piping by serging fine pearl, bead, or sequin strands** to a folded strip of 1-1/4" organza or *Seams Great* (Fig. 6-29).

✎ **Note:** When serging over sequin strands, make sure the sequins overlap away from the machine .

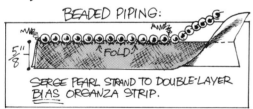

Fig. 6-29

1. **Adjust for a balanced stitch, slightly longer than the pearl or bead diameter.** Use fine #80 monofilament nylon thread in the upper looper and matching serger thread in the needle and lower looper. The stitch width should barely cover the strand. (A rolled-edge stitch works well for fine bead or pearl trim. Use a long, wide balanced stitch for sequin strands.)

2. Slowly serge the strand to the fold, **over the front and under the back of the foot;** it may be necessary to remove the foot.

3. Hide the looper threads between the beads, pearls, or sequins.

☞ **Special Tip:** Look for the new bead trim applicator feet that are now available from some serger manufacturers. Grooved on top of the front and the underside of the back, they are designed for effortless application of pearl or bead strands. One brand is also fingerless, like the foot shown, to prevent any interference with the strand (Fig. 6-30).

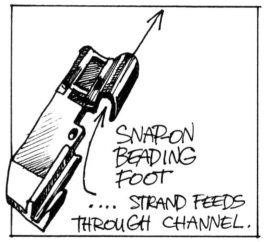

Fig. 6-30

Traced Tulle

Serging is a splendid finish for tulle veils, headpieces, accessories, and accents (Fig. 6-31). **To trace the edge, simply serge with a narrow rolled-edge stitch.** Experiment with different threads—rayon thread in the upper looper adds shine to the edge, whereas woolly stretch nylon provides denser coverage and a matte finish. **Serge**

over fishline to flounce the tulle tracing; stretch after serging (see page 104).

Fig. 6-31

For embellished tracing, serge a pearl strand to the edge. Many brides choose this finish for their blusher veil, which covers only the face; the pearl strand adds weight as well as decoration.

To coordinate bridesmaid headpieces, serge-finish tulle with thread the color of their dresses. Tie into a big bow and glue or sew to a brimmed hat for an inexpensive headpiece.

A traced tulle headpiece (Fig. 6-32) is easy-to-make and very popular.

1. **Cut out** the tulle, as shown (Fig. 6-33).

Fig. 6-32

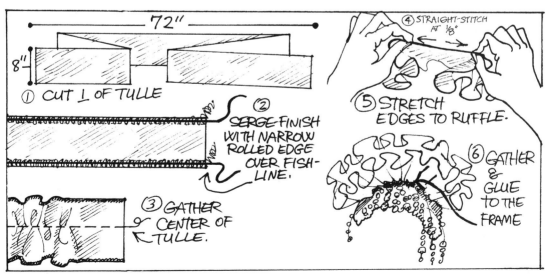

① CUT ⊥ OF TULLE

② SERGE FINISH WITH NARROW ROLLED EDGE OVER FISH-LINE.

③ GATHER CENTER OF TULLE.

④ STRAIGHT-STITCH AT ⅛"

⑤ STRETCH EDGES TO RUFFLE.

⑥ GATHER & GLUE TO THE FRAME

Fig. 6-33

2. **Serge-finish the longer edges** over fishline.

3. **Gather the center of the tulle strip** (save time by using a gathering foot); draw up the gathering to fit the headpiece frame.

4. **Fold the gathered strip,** right sides together, along the gathering line. **Straight-stitch 1/8" from the fold** so that the strip will stand up.

5. **Stretch the traced edges** to increase the flouncing.

6. **Attach to the headpiece** with a glue gun.

Easiest Serging Order

The serger has revolutionized formal and bridal sewing—the neat, fast stitching and cutting indisputably transcend the zigzag finishing once common to home-sewn garments. Read through the pattern guide sheet before planning the optimum order.

• **Determine the type of seam and seam finish.**

• **Use the flat order of construction** (sew or serge in a circle after completing as much edge-finishing, facing, and hemming as possible).

• **Maximize machine sewing** and eliminate handsewing whenever possible.

Quick Tips

Quick Slip Tip

Create a custom slip easily and inexpensively. Simply sew tiers of crinoline ruffles (see Serged Ruffles, pages 103 – 105) to a pull-on half-slip. Most slip ruffles are about 12" deep and at least twice the slip circumference.

For heavier gown fabrics, cut the ruffles double-layer; for lighter fabrics, cut the ruffles single-layer and finish the edges with serged tracing or lace trim. Layer the ruffles as necessary to hold the skirt silhouette.

☞ **Special Tip:** To hem accurately, put on the slip and use it as a guide when marking the skirt length.

Other Quick Tips

• If you need several of the same dresses or gowns for a group, **your best bet is to have one person do all the cutting out and sewing.** Then, for the special event, or particularly for photographs, all the garments will look and fit similarly.

• Fit the garment in two steps. (Of course, the ideal is to fit after each seam is stitched, but this isn't always feasible or time-efficient.)

First, fit the bodice with the lining glued in position (see Timesaving Bodice Techniques, page 98). Altering is easy because the seams are not serged. **Do the second fitting after the skirt has been seamed and sewn to the bodice so that you can mark the hem.** Wear the proper shoes, slip, and undergarments to assess the fit accurately.

• **Clean and oil** both your sewing machine and serger before starting the project. After oiling, **be certain to wipe off any excess oil,** which can permanently spot the fabric.

• **For easy gathering with your sewing**

machine, adjust for a long stitch length and tighten the needle tension. Stitch on the seamline or where you want the gathering.

• Use *ThreadFuse* in the lower looper when serge-seaming. Carefully press the narrow seam to one side to eliminate the need for topstitching. Serge-finish the edge of the garment or gloves with *ThreadFuse* in the upper looper. The lace trim can be pressed to the edge, eliminating gluing or topstitching.

• The wiry metallic threads may show through the stitching on the rolled edge of metallic fabrics, especially if serging on a bias edge. Widen the bite to the right to allow more fabric to roll under.

• When serging a rolled edge on metallic fabrics, the stitching may pull from the edge. Eliminate this by lengthening the stitch. If the stitching pulls off when serge-seaming metallic fabrics, reinforce the seam by straight-stitching next to the serged needle line.

Project: Fingerless Gloves

Leftover fabric can be used to make these classic fingerless gloves. Even though you'll be using a commercial pattern, it's important to try on and, if necessary, alter the gloves for the sleekest fit.

1. **Cut out the gloves** using a commercial pattern (check the bridal tab of fabric-store catalogs). Flexible tulles and laces contour beautifully to fit wrists and hands. Measure and pin-fit to check the size.

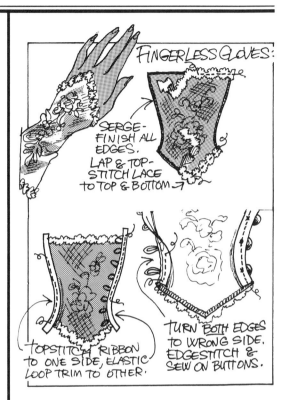

Fig. 6-34

2. **Serge-finish** the edges (Fig. 6-34).

3. **Glue and topstitch lace trim** to the top and bottom edges.

4. On one long side, **topstitch elastic loop trim.** Turn to the wrong side and edge-stitch. **Note:** Elastic loop trim is sold by the yard in most fabric stores that carry bridal supplies. If you cannot locate this trim in your area, write to the mail-order companies specializing in wedding fabrics and notions listed in the Fabrics-by-Mail Directory at the end of the book.

5. On the other long side, **topstitch 1/8" ribbon over the serging.** Press 1/8" to the wrong side and edge-stitch. Sew on buttons spaced to fit the elastic loops.

7. Serging Denim, Canvas, and Tapestry

Denims and tapestries are not only durable and versatile, but both are fashionable and fun, yet functional. Classic canvas, known for its durability, makes its appearance year after year in bags, belts, and other accessories. With simple serging techniques, these fabrics are fast and fun to sew.

Fabric Choices

Denim

This durable twill fabric is identified by colored (most often blue) and white diagonal lines on both the front and the back of the fabric. Originally denim was made only of 100% cotton, but now blends of cotton/polyester or cotton/*Lycra* are readily available in a variety of colors and weights.

Canvas

Canvas is a heavy, durable fabric that is often stiffer than denim. Because the fabric is a plain weave with no discernible right or wrong side, it works well for self-fabric bindings. Canvas is made of cotton or linen and is most often available in an unbleached off-white.

Tapestry

This ornamental or decorative fabric is popular for vests, jackets, skirts, and accessories. Tapestry is a less durable, but heavier, fabric with an extra set of yarns on the surface, giving it a floral or embroidered look. Tapestries are available in a variety of fibers and weights and in many patterns and colors.

Pattern Selection

For denims, select a casual style. Choose lighter-weight denims for gathered or pleated designs. Decorative trims, such as satins, velvets, metallics, sequins, and embroidery, will add sophistication and flair to a casual design. Whether the garment style is casual or dressy, **denim lends itself well to topstitching.**

Canvas is used most often for bags or belts, but lighter-weight canvas can also be used for casual jackets. Because the fabric is bulky and stiff, select a pattern with few seams and one that requires little easing.

Tapestry is popular in designs varying from casual to very dressy. Select a design with little seaming and detail to avoid detracting from the decorative fabric (Fig. 7-1). Tapestry vests, like the one shown on the facing page, are a good choice.

Because these fabrics are bulkier than most, **use an extended facing instead of a sew-on facing to reduce seam thickness** (Fig. 7-2).

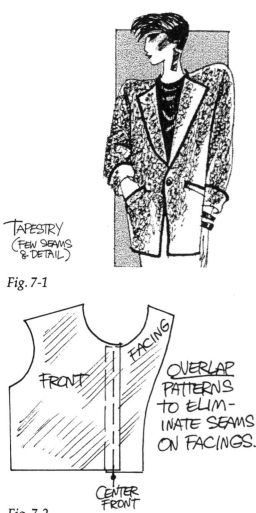

TAPESTRY
(FEW SEAMS
& DETAIL)

Fig. 7-1

FRONT FACING

OVERLAP
PATTERNS
TO ELIM-
INATE SEAMS
ON FACINGS.

CENTER
FRONT

Fig. 7-2

Timesaving Notions

 Note: For more notions information, refer to the general Timesaving Notions section in the Introduction and the Notions Guidelines for Specialty Fabrics chart on page *x*. Notions with fabric-specific explanations are explained here.

• **Scissors or rotary cutter and mat**

• **Pattern weights**

• **Machine needles**

• **Pins**

• **All-purpose or serger thread**

• **Buttonhole twist, pearl cotton, or pearl rayon** (Fig. 7-3)

• *ThreadFuse*

USE DECORATIVE THREAD
IN BOTH LOOPERS WHEN
BOTH SIDES OF THE EDGE
WILL BE EXPOSED.

Fig. 7-3

• **Woolly stretch nylon**

• **Marking pen**—Because tapestry fabrics are prone to water spotting, never use water-soluble marking pens.

Interfacing

Fusible woven or nonwoven interfacing can be used for heavier fabrics. Select an interfacing designed for medium- to heavy-weight fabrics. For heavy-weight denim and canvas, **interfacing may not be necessary** because the fabric provides its own stability.

Lining

Lining is not necessary to stabilize these durable fabrics. It can be used, however, to give a more finished appearance on the inside of the garment.

• **Lining the inside of a tapestry garment will eliminate pulled yarns that occur during wear.**

• To eliminate bulk, **lining fabric may be used to face collars, cuffs, waistbands, and pockets.**

• **Select a lining fabric that has washing requirements compatible with the garment fabric.** For example, use a washable lining for denim and a dry-cleanable lining for tapestries.

Fabric Preparation

Before pretreating, **serge-finish the raw ends of the fabric to prevent raveling** (Fig. 7-4).

Denim

Because denim will shrink, **pretreat it by laundering several times.** Laundering will ensure complete preshrinkage and will soften the stiff fabric.

Canvas

Pretreating canvas may remove the finish and give the fabric a worn look. **Consider how you will use the item** to

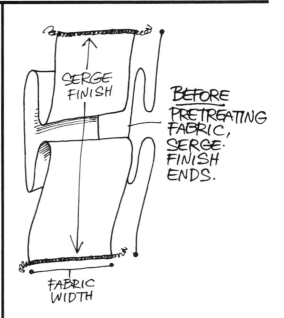

Fig. 7-4

determine if shrinkage will be a problem, and if pretreating is necessary.

Tapestry

Tapestries should be dry cleaned only. Because they shrink and can be damaged in the cleaning process, **do not pretreat them.** When cleaning the finished garment, do only spot cleaning, if possible.

Pattern Layout and Cutting

Lay out denims and tapestries with the nap. Canvas may be cut in either direction.

Check for repeat designs on the tapestry fabric. Use weights instead of pins to avoid snagging the fabric when cutting out.

Pressing

Press denims and canvas with a steam iron set at high heat. Press from the wrong side to avoid glazing the fabric.

When Pressing Tapestry Fabric:

• To avoid damaging or shrinking the fabric, **test** the temperature and steam by pressing on the wrong side of scraps.

• **Use a well-padded surface or a terry towel to prevent flattening the fabric surface.**

• **Place strips of paper between seam allowances or darts and the garment fabric** to avoid leaving an imprint on the right side of the garment (Fig. 7-5).

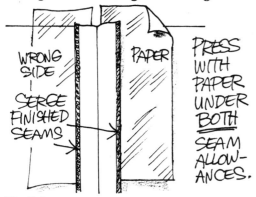

Fig. 7-5

Seams and Seam Finishes

These heavy fabrics usually fray easily. Serging will finish the edges professionally and prevent raveling. For the heaviest fabrics, you may have to **reinforce seams with straight-stitching for durability.**

• When sewing tapestry fabric, **do all fitting before stitching.** Ripping out

stitches might damage the fabric.

• **Use a medium stitch length (3.5mm) and loosen the tensions slightly** to avoid puckered seams.

• Because tapestry fabric may shift while seaming, **pin frequently with the pins parallel to the seam but just inside the seam allowance.**

• **Use taut sewing** by holding both layers of fabric taut in front of and behind the needle, without pulling. Or use your differential feed set below 1.0.

For Durable Inside Seaming of Heavier Fabrics
(not decorative outside seams)

• **Serge-finish the fabric edges.** Then **straight-stitch with a 5/8" seam allowance and press the seams open.** Top-stitch 1/4" on both sides of the seamline to secure the seam allowances (Fig. 7-6).

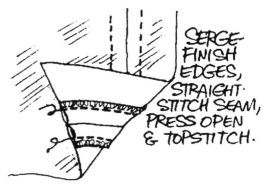

Fig. 7-6

• For a **mock flat-felled seam, straight-stitch the seam with a 5/8" seam allowance.** Adjust to a wide, medium-length and balanced 3- or 3/4-thread stitch. Serge the seam allowances together, close to the seamline, trimming as you serge. Press the seam allowances to one side. From the right side, **topstitch** close to the fold and, again, 1/4" from the first topstitching (Fig. 7-7).

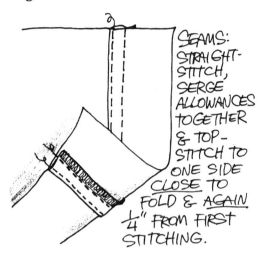

SEAMS: STRAIGHT-STITCH, SERGE ALLOWANCES TOGETHER & TOP-STITCH TO ONE SIDE CLOSE TO FOLD & AGAIN 1/4" FROM FIRST STITCHING.

Fig. 7-7

• **Another mock flat-felled seaming method uses *ThreadFuse* in the lower looper.** After serging the seam allowances together, press them to one side and fuse them in place. Topstitch as above with two rows of topstitching.

For Decoratively Serged Seams on the Outside of a Garment

• **Test denims and canvas for durability and raveling.** Serge a 6" test seam, then wash and dry it to check for raveling. If the fabric ravels, try shortening the stitch length and test again.

• When the serged seam is on the outside of the garment, **your stitching must be top-quality and tensions must be set accurately.** To prevent uneven stitches, nothing should inter-fere with the even feeding of the looper threads (Fig. 7-8).

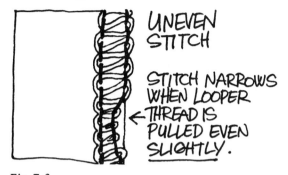

UNEVEN STITCH

STITCH NARROWS WHEN LOOPER ← THREAD IS PULLED EVEN SLIGHTLY.

Fig. 7-8

• Thread the serger with decorative or contrasting thread in the upper looper and all-purpose or serger thread in the needle and lower looper. Another option is to use *ThreadFuse* in the lower looper. When making a lapped seam, use *ThreadFuse* in the lower looper on the upper layer of fabric only (the layer that will be lapped over the other).

• Plan which direction to stitch so that the decorative thread will be on top when you press the seams toward the back. **With a wide, short and balanced 3- or 3/4-thread stitch, serge-seam the edges wrong sides together, trimming the seam allowance.** Press the seam allowances to one side and edge-stitch (Fig. 7-9). Press all seams toward the back for consistency.

• For lapped seams, **serge-finish each edge separately,** right side up, **trimming off 3/8" of the 5/8" seam allowance. Overlap the serged-finished edges, matching the seamlines.** Lap and edge-stitch as shown (Fig. 7-10).

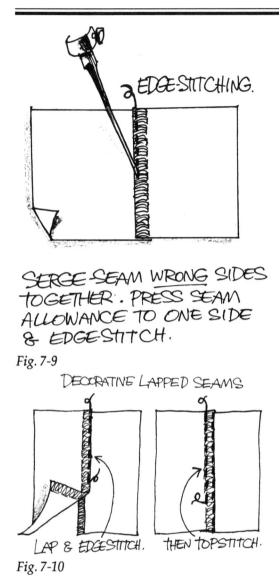

a EDGE-STITCHING.

SERGE SEAM WRONG SIDES
TOGETHER. PRESS SEAM
ALLOWANCE TO ONE SIDE
& EDGESTITCH.

Fig. 7-9

DECORATIVE LAPPED SEAMS

LAP & EDGESTITCH.   THEN TOPSTITCH.

Fig. 7-10

Edge Finishing

Decorative Self Binding

To decoratively self-bind stable denim and canvas (allow 7/8" for a hem allowance), follow these steps:

1. Use decorative thread in the upper looper. **With the wrong side up, serge-finish the edge** using a wide,

short and balanced 3- or 3/4-thread stitch (Fig. 7-11).

DECORATIVELY SERGED SELF-BINDING:

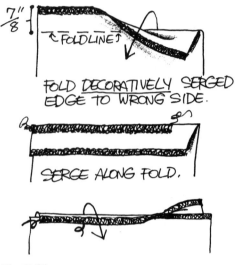

7/8" ↕ *FOLDLINE*

FOLD *DECORATIVELY* SERGED EDGE TO WRONG SIDE.

SERGE ALONG FOLD.

Fig. 7-11

2. **Fold the serged edge 7/8" to the wrong side.** Rethread the upper looper with all-purpose or serger thread and, using a wide, medium-length stitch, **serge the fold** without cutting it off.

3. **Fold the decoratively serged edge to the right side (encasing the serged seam). Edge-stitch.**

Faux-Braid Finishing

Faux-braid finishing is perfect for durable fabrics (Fig. 7-12). Before serging on the garment, always test and refine the finishing technique on scraps of fabric first.

1. **Press 3/8" to 1/2" to the wrong side.**

2. **Topstitch 1/8" from the fold,** using a long stitch (8 stitches/inch).

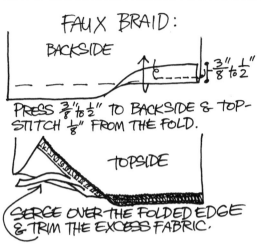

FAUX BRAID:
BACKSIDE

PRESS ⅜" to ½" TO BACKSIDE & TOP-
STITCH ⅛" FROM THE FOLD.

TOPSIDE

SERGE OVER THE FOLDED EDGE
& TRIM THE EXCESS FABRIC.

Fig. 7-12

3. Thread the serger with decorative thread in the upper looper and adjust for a narrow, medium-length (2.5 to 3mm) and balanced 3-thread stitch. From the right side, **serge slowly over the folded edge,** but do not cut the fold.

4. On the wrong side, **trim the excess fabric close to the serging.**

Faux-Braid Variation

For the faux-braid variation, follow Steps 1, 2, and 3 above. In Step 3, serge over two or three strands of filler cord, such as topstitching thread or crochet thread (Fig. 7-13). Use the following tips for the faux-braid variation.

• **Position the filler cord over the front and under the back of the foot,** between the knife and the needle.

• **Pull on the filler cord to ease in the serged edge.** This is especially helpful when serge-finishing a curve.

• When finished, weave the filler-cord tails under the serging, using a tapestry needle or loop turner.

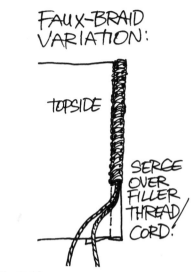

**FAUX-BRAID
VARIATION:**

TOPSIDE

SERGE
OVER
FILLER
THREAD/
CORD!

Fig. 7-13

Fast Hems

For easiest hemming, **serge-finish the edge** and finish the hem using one of the following methods:

• With denims and canvas, turn 5/8" to the wrong side. For a durable hem, **topstitch close to the fold and again 1/4" from the first stitching** (Fig. 7-14). Use *ThreadFuse* in the lower looper when serge-finishing; then fuse the hem into position and topstitch.

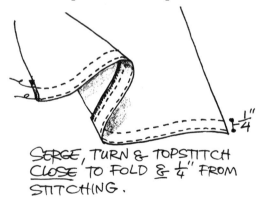

SERGE, TURN & TOPSTITCH
CLOSE TO FOLD & ¼" FROM
STITCHING.

Fig. 7-14

- For a deeper jacket hem, press the desired hem allowance to the wrong side and **machine blindstitch or hand-stitch to secure** (Fig. 7-15).

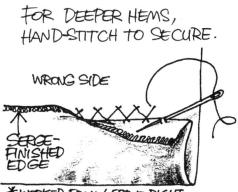

FOR DEEPER HEMS, HAND-STITCH TO SECURE.

WRONG SIDE

SERGE-FINISHED EDGE

* WORKED FROM <u>LEFT</u> TO RIGHT.

Fig. 7-15

Special Techniques

The Hip Slimming Elastic Gusset

Elastic gussets used in more-rigid denims will add to a garment's comfort and fit. Gussets are inserted in the outseams from the waistline to the upper hipline. The wide elastic used by most ready-to-wear manufacturers is now readily available to home-sewers.

Elastic gussets may be incorporated into a pattern or added to a ready-made garment (Fig. 7-16). They are easily used on patterns with high, bandless waistlines. When adding a gusset to a pleated-front style, the gusset length should be the same or shorter than the pleat stitching; if it's longer, the elastic can skew the pleat toward the outseam.

Wide, 3" elastic often has one ruffled edge; this is the type and width sold by

THE HIP SLIMMING ELASTIC GUSSET!

Fig. 7-16

many fabric retailers and by mail-order suppliers. Color selection available to both home-sewers and manufacturers is limited to basics—red, black, white, and navy.

Pattern Preparation

To prepare the pattern, trim 1-1/2" from the outseams, as shown (Fig. 7-17). (With elastic gussets added, the finished waist measurement of the garment will be 2" less than the pattern waist measurement. The elastic stretches to compensate for the smaller fit.)

Easy Gusset How-tos

For two 3"-wide (finished) triangular gussets, you will need a 30" length of

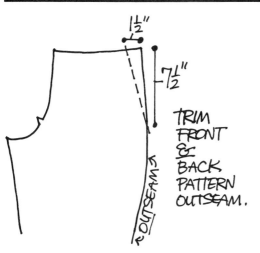

Fig. 7-17

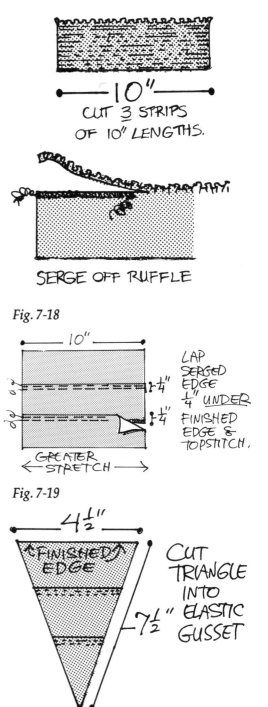

CUT 3 STRIPS OF 10" LENGTHS.

SERGE OFF RUFFLE

Fig. 7-18

Fig. 7-19

Fig. 7-20

elastic. The greater stretch of the elastic will go **around** the body, so the elastic must be pieced horizontally. (Piecing is seen in ready-to-wear elastic gussets, too.)

1. **Cut the elastic into three 10" strips.** Before piecing the elastic, **serge off the ruffled edge** with a medium to wide stitch width and a medium stitch length, as shown (Fig. 7-18).

2. **Lap the serged edge of one strip 1/4" under a finished edge of one of the other strips. Stretching as you sew, topstitch with two rows of machine stitching** (1/8" apart) **to secure the seam.** Repeat for the other elastic strip, as shown (Fig. 7-19).

3. For 3"-wide finished gussets, **cut two gusset triangles from** the pieced elastic—4-1/2" wide at the upper finished edge by **7-1/2" long at the sides** (Fig. 7-20).

4. With right sides together, **place the gusset on the garment front, aligning the finished edge with the waistline**

seam. Straight-stitch with a 5/8" seam allowance. With a medium to wide stitch width and medium stitch length, serge the seam allowances together (Fig. 7-21).

5. With right sides together, **place the other side of the gusset on the back of the garment, aligning the finished edge of elastic with the waistline seam** (Fig. 7-21). Straight-stitch with a 5/8" seam allowance, continuing to the pant hem. With a medium to wide stitch width and medium stitch length, serge the seam allowances together.

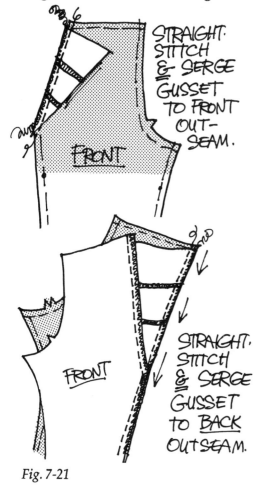

STRAIGHT-
STITCH
& SERGE
GUSSET
TO FRONT
OUT-
SEAM.

STRAIGHT-
STITCH
& SERGE
GUSSET
TO BACK
OUTSEAM.

Fig. 7-21

6. Press the seam allowances away from the gusset and edge-stitch (Fig. 7-22).

PRESS SEAMS AWAY FROM GUSSET & EDGESTITCH CONVENTIONALLY.

Fig. 7-22

7. Finish the garment following the pattern instructions. Face the part of the top waistline edge that is not elasticized.

Gusseting Ready-made Pants

Rip out the outseams to 12" below the waistline edge. Recut the side seam as shown in Fig. 7-17. Then follow the Easy Gusset How-to's.

Quick Tips

• **To further soften and give the popular used appearance** to denim, pretreat by adding to the wash water 1/2 cup of chlorine bleach for every two yards of denim. Add the bleach to each laundry cycle during the preshrinking process.

• **To prevent the denim from fading while pretreating,** add 1/2 cup of vinegar to the wash water for every two yards of denim. Repeat each time the fabric is pretreated. After the garment is completed, turn it inside out when laundering or have it dry cleaned.

• To prevent shrinkage of denim garments, **remove them from the dryer while damp.** Pull on the seams to straighten and allow them to air-dry.

• When serging with heavier decorative threads, **use a large (size 90/14) needle to prevent skipped stitches. Loosen the upper looper tension** or remove the thread from a thread guide or the tension disc to allow better coverage.

Project: Quick-and-Easy Canvas Bathroom Organizer

(Fig. 7-23)

Fig. 7-23

Materials needed

• 3/4 yard of 45" canvas (will make three organizers)

• Matching or contrasting decorative thread for faux-braiding

• One 20" wooden dowel

• 1 yard of cording

1. Cut one rectangle 18" wide by 27" long from the canvas fabric. With matching thread in both loopers, **serge-finish both long edges** with a wide, short and balanced 3- or 3/4-thread stitch (Fig. 7-24).

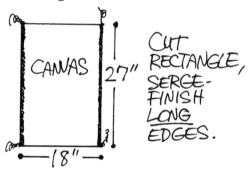

Fig. 7-24

2. **Create a faux-braid finish on both short ends** (refer back to Figure 7-12). Press the upper edge 1/2" toward the wrong side and the lower edge 1/2" toward the right side (Fig. 7-25). Top-stitch 1/8" from the folds, using a long stitch (8 stitches/inch). With decorative thread in the upper looper, adjust for a narrow, medium-length (2.5 to 3mm) and balanced 3-thread stitch. From the right side, serge slowly over the folded edges, but do not cut the folds. Trim the excess fabric close to the serging on both ends.

3. Fold the rectangle in half, wrong sides together, and **topstitch 1" from**

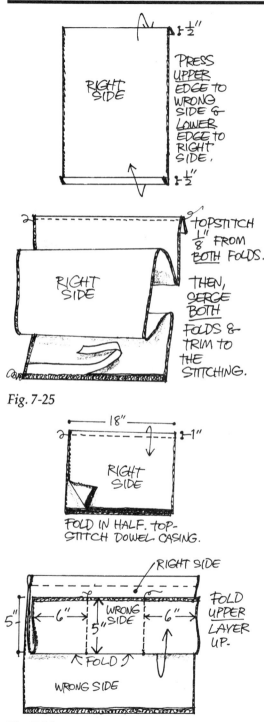

Fig. 7-25

(Figure annotations:)
RIGHT SIDE

PRESS UPPER EDGE TO WRONG SIDE & LOWER EDGE TO RIGHT SIDE.

$1\frac{1}{2}''$

$1\frac{1}{2}''$

RIGHT SIDE

topstitch $\frac{1}{8}''$ FROM BOTH FOLDS.

THEN, SERGE BOTH FOLDS & TRIM TO THE STITCHING.

18''

$1''$

RIGHT SIDE

FOLD IN HALF. TOP-STITCH DOWEL CASING.

Fig. 7-26

RIGHT SIDE

5''

6''

WRONG SIDE

5''

6''

FOLD

FOLD UPPER LAYER UP.

WRONG SIDE

the folded edge to form the dowel casing (Fig. 7-26).

4. **Fold the upper layer up 6" and topstitch two vertical seams 6" from each side through all layers,** as shown (Fig. 7-26).

5. **Fold the underlayer up 4-1/2" so that it overlaps the lower edge of the upper pockets. Then topstitch three vertical seams approximately 4-1/2" apart** (Fig. 7-27).

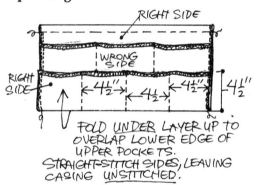

(Figure annotations:)
RIGHT SIDE
WRONG SIDE
RIGHT SIDE
$4\frac{1}{2}''$ $4\frac{1}{2}''$ $4\frac{1}{2}''$ $4\frac{1}{2}''$
FOLD UNDER LAYER UP TO OVERLAP LOWER EDGE OF UPPER POCKETS. STRAIGHT-STITCH SIDES, LEAVING CASING UNSTITCHED.

Fig. 7-27

6. **Straight-stitch the side edges, through all layers,** leaving the casing unstitched.

7. **Insert the dowel. Cut the cording into two 18" pieces.** Tie the cording at each end of the dowel and attach it to a towel bar (Fig. 7-28).

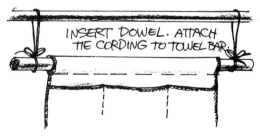

(Figure annotations:)
INSERT DOWEL. ATTACH TIE CORDING TO TOWEL BAR.

Fig. 7-28

Specialty Fabrics

8. *Pile Fabric Know-How*

Pile fabrics, from casual corduroys and terry cloth to more elegant velvets and velveteens, have often presented an unsurpassable challenge to the home-sewer. Sewing with these fabrics can be frustrating because they tend to slip and ravel. Now, using simply serged techniques, they can be finished quickly and easily with minimal effort.

Fabric Choices

Pile fabrics are three-dimensional because they have extra yarns incorporated over the surface of the fabric, forming the pile. The pile can be cut (as in corduroy), sheared (as in velveteen and velvet), or uncut (as in the loops in terry cloth).

The quality of the fabric depends on how tightly the base fabric is woven and on the density of the pile. Determine the quality by folding the fabric back on itself with the wrong sides together. A low-density pile will allow the base fabric to show through. In a tightly woven fabric, the pile will not pull out or snag easily, making it more durable. In addition, it is easier to sew because it will ravel less.

Corduroy

(Fig. 8-1)

Fig. 8-1

This heavy, durable fabric is usually made from cotton or cotton-blend. Corduroy is identified by its wales or ribs, which are made when the pile is cut and brushed. Corduroy is available in various wale widths, from a narrow pinwale to a wide 1/4"

wale. A midwale is the easiest to sew and the most readily available. Corduroy can be plain or patterned.

Choose corduroy for durable children's clothing or for casual sportswear.

Velveteen

(Fig. 8-2)

Fig. 8-2

Velveteen is a medium-weight fabric with a short, sheared pile and a smooth surface. Velveteen is made from long-staple cotton or cotton and polyester fibers. It is easier to sew and has more body than velvet. Differentiate between velvet and velveteen by folding the fabric. Velveteen breaks in a crosswise row and velvet breaks in a lengthwise row (Fig. 8-3).

Velveteen is very versatile and can be used for casual garments or elegant eveningwear.

Velvet

(Fig. 8-4)

Velvet is a soft, luxurious fabric with a flat, dense, sheared pile and a smooth surface. Available in various weights, velvet is made from shorter-

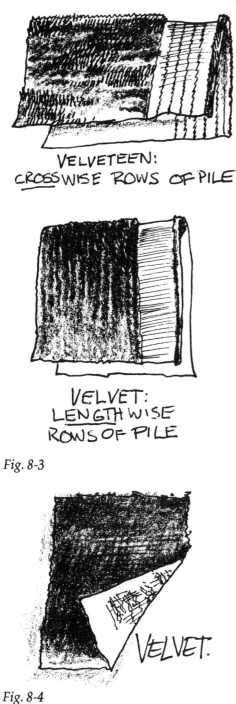

VELVETEEN:
<u>CROSS</u>WISE ROWS OF PILE

VELVET:
<u>LENGTH</u>WISE
ROWS OF PILE

Fig. 8-3

VELVET.

Fig. 8-4

filament silk, rayon, and cotton fibers (in contrast to the long staple fibers of velveteen). Velvet has more drapeability than velveteen and also is more lustrous. Velvet and velveteen are not wound on the usual bolts but are attached to special bolts so the fabric will not crease and the pile will not flatten.

Choose velvet for special-occasion garments because of its luster and drapeability. Cotton velvet is well suited for children's dressy clothes because it is washable.

Terry Cloth
(Fig. 8-5)

TERRY CLOTH.

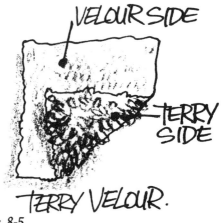

VELOUR SIDE

TERRY SIDE

TERRY VELOUR.

Fig. 8-5

Terry cloth is a medium- to heavy-weight cotton or cotton/polyester fabric with looped or uncut pile. Terry velour has a looped pile surface on one side and a cut pile surface on the other side. The quality of terry fabrics varies, so choose a tightly woven fabric with a dense pile for ease in sewing. For more absorbency, select 100% cotton fabric.

Terry is well suited for casual garments, beach coverups, towels, and robes.

Pattern Selection

When choosing a pattern for pile fabrics, look for the following:

• **Select a simple design with a minimum of seams and darts.** Use an extended facing, instead of a sew-on facing, to reduce the bulk of seams. Corresponding straight seams on pattern pieces can be eliminated by overlapping pattern pieces at the seamlines (Fig. 8-6). Convert the center back and front seamlines to foldlines. This will minimize bulk and save sewing time.

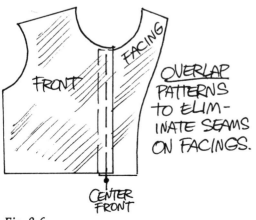

Fig. 8-6

• When sewing with velvets and velveteens, **avoid designs with top-stitching and buttonholes.** Any outside stitching will flatten the pile.

• **Velvets and lightweight corduroys lend themselves well to soft, drapeable designs.**

Timesaving Notions

✎ **Note:** For more notions information, refer to the general Timesaving Notions section in the Introduction and the Notions Guidelines for Specialty Fabrics chart on page *x*. Notions with fabric-specific explanations are explained here.

• **Scissors**

• **Pattern weights**

• **Machine needles**

• **Pins**—Avoid using silk pins in velvet because they are not the finest size. Take care when pinning velvet. Pins will leave holes, so do any pinning inside the seamline. Substitute fine-sized needles for pins when you must pin into the garment.

• **All-purpose or serger thread**

• *ThreadFuse*

• **Woolly stretch nylon**

• **Marking pen**—Test air-erasable pens on fabric scraps before marking **even the wrong side** of your garment. Do not use water-soluble pens on pile fabrics; these fabrics are prone to water spotting.

Interfacing

Terry cloth, corduroy, and velveteen can be interfaced with a fusible interfacing. Test various fusibles on scraps of actual garment fabric to see if the pile becomes flattened while fusing.

• Pretreat fusible interfacing by steam-shrinking it after cutting, just prior to fusing. Here's how:

1. Press the fashion-fabric where the interfacing will be applied. Then position the interfacing, resin side down.

2. Hold the steam iron an inch above the interfacing and steam generously for a few seconds. Use the burst-of-steam feature on your iron, if you have it. You can often see the edges of the interfacing draw up slightly as you steam; the slight change in size due to shrinking does not affect the finished product.

• **To apply fusible interfacing:**

1. **Cover the pressing surface with a heavy terry towel or an extra piece of velveteen.**

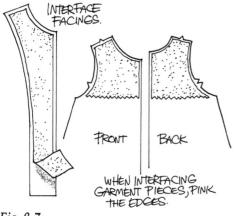

Fig. 8-7

2. **Interface the facing pieces rather than the garment pieces** to eliminate any lines that might show on the outside of the garment (Fig. 8-7). If you must interface a garment, pink the edges to avoid any telltale line.

✎ **Note:** Interface velvets with a sew-in woven or nonwoven interfacing slightly lighter-weight than the fabric.

Lining

Corduroy, velvet, and velveteens wear better if the garment is lined. Lining reduces wrinkling and helps the garment slide on and off more easily.

✎ **Note:** Terry cloth does not need to be lined.

Fabric Preparation

To prevent shrinkage after construction, pretreat the fabric before cutting it out (shrinkage could cause puckered seams). Pretreating will also remove finishes, which can cause skipped stitches. **Pretreat with the same method you'll use to clean the garment.** Take care not to flatten the pile during the cleaning process.

Cut pile looks best if dry cleaned. **Cotton corduroy and velveteens will fade with laundering and will look worn.** When pretreating, keep the garment use in mind. Fabrics used in children's garments may be laundered and machine dried for softness, while fabric used in a jacket or skirt should be dry cleaned.

Pattern Layout and Cutting

✎ **Note:** Velvet usually comes in a 39" width, which often is not listed in the yardage requirements on the back of the pattern envelope. **Lay out the pattern at the store or at home before purchasing the fabric.**

Layout Tips

Use the "with nap" layout. During the manufacture of the fabric, the pile is pressed in one direction. The direction of the pile will change the appearance of the fabric. The fabric may be cut with the nap running either up or down.

Cutting with the nap running up enhances the fabric's beauty; however, the garment wears best with the nap running down. **Always make sure that the pile runs in the same direction throughout the garment,** regardless of the overall direction. When the naps do not run in the same direction, the garment will appear to be made of two different colors of fabric.

• **Determine the direction of the nap or pile by running your hand over the fabric.** If you have trouble determining the direction of the nap, wrap the fabric over your shoulders and determine the nap direction by noting the difference in color.

• **When the fabric feels rough, the nap is running up** and the color will appear darker and richer.

• **When the fabric feels smooth, the nap is running down** and the fabric will appear lighter in color and shinier.

• Mark the direction of the pile with chalk on the back side of the fabric close to the selvage edge (Fig. 8-8). **Be sure to cut all pieces in the same direction.**

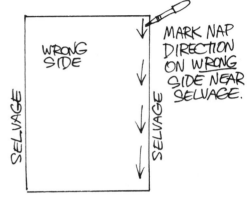

Fig. 8-8

• **Lay out the collar, cuffs, belt, and waistband on the crosswise grain** so the direction of the nap will not be noticeable.

Cutting Tips

• **Use pattern weights** when cutting out, and **cut with the direction of the pile.**

• Eliminate bulk in the garment by cutting neckline, collar, cuff, and pocket facings from a lighter-weight, firmly woven fabric.

• **Cut corduroy and velveteen with the fabric folded right sides together** (Fig. 8-9).

• To prevent slippage when cutting out velvet, cut it out single-layer, **reversing the pattern when cutting the second piece** (Fig. 8-9).

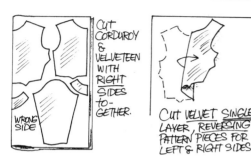

Fig. 8-9

- Match the wales of corduroy as you would match stripes.

Pressing

For corduroy, velveteen, and velvet, press with a minimum of pressure or with none at all. The fabric will appear lighter in color if the pile is flattened. Here are some tips:

- Use a steam iron for pressing. For pressing seams, use only the point of the iron. Never place the surface of the iron on the garment.

- Place strips of paper between seam allowances or darts and the garment fabric (Fig. 8-10). This will help prevent leaving an imprint on the right side of the garment.

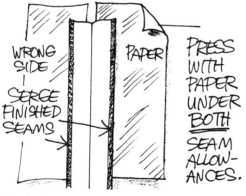

Fig. 8-10

- **Always press from the wrong side and in the direction of the nap** (Fig. 8-11). Without touching the iron to the fabric, steam the hems well. Then finger-press.

Fig. 8-11

- When pressing velvets and velveteens, **use a needle board to avoid flattening the pile.** Or use a piece of self-fabric on the pressing surface.

- **Press velvet from the wrong side using a low temperature setting and a press cloth.**

- **Terry cloth requires very little pressing.** Press from the wrong side of the garment. No other special pressing precautions are necessary. If the pile is flattened, steam it well, then finger-brush to fluff up the nap.

Seams and Seam Finishes

Corduroy and Velveteens

When seaming two layers of pile fabric, the upper layer has a tendency to slip, causing the under layer to pucker. The longer feed dogs of the serger eliminate some of the fabric shifting. Sergers will also neatly finish the ravelly edges characteristic of pile fabrics.

• **Use a medium stitch length (3.5mm) and loosen the tensions slightly** to avoid any puckering of the seams.

• Because the fabric shifts, **pin frequently with the pins parallel to the seam** and just outside the seam allowance (Fig. 8-12).

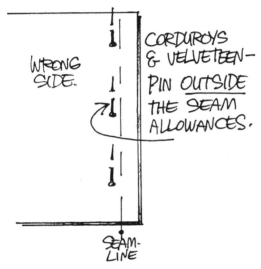

Fig. 8-12

• **Use taut serging** by stretching both layers of fabric in front of and behind the needle **without pulling** the fabric through (Fig. 8-13). Or use the smallest number (less than 1.0) on your differential feed.

• **Reduce the pressure on the presser foot.** Lighter pressure will eliminate flattening the pile and leaving an imprint from the presser foot on the fabric.

• **Serge with the nap** in the lengthwise direction.

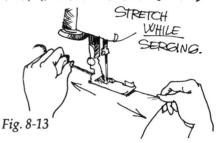

Fig. 8-13

Velvet

Do all fitting before stitching. Removed stitches may leave holes in the velvet.

Layers of velvet fabric often slip during sewing, even more than other pile fabrics. For easier sewing and serging, follow these guidelines.

• **Pin inside the seam allowances,** making sure to remove the pins before they reach the knives (Fig. 8-14).

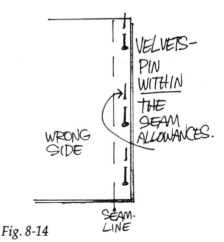

Fig. 8-14

• Hold the **under** layer of velvet taut to prevent slippage (Fig. 8-15).

• When seaming, **serge or sew a few inches at a time, then raise the presser foot and readjust the fabric layers.**

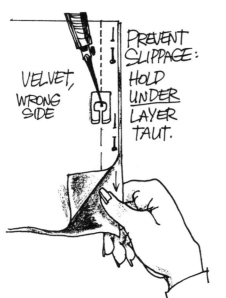

Fig. 8-15

• When seaming velvet to another, smoother fabric, **sew or serge with the velvet on the top.**

Terry Cloth

Terry cloth requires very little adjustment while serging. The seams will not slip as in other pile fabrics. To seam the terry:

• **Straight-stitch the seam with a 5/8" seam allowance. Adjust for a wide, medium-length and balanced 3- or 3/4-thread stitch** (Fig. 8-16). **Serge the seam allowances together, close to the seamline, trimming as you serge.**

Fig. 8-16

• For tightly woven terry fabric or for garments with little stress on the seams, **adjust for a shorter-length (2.5mm), widest-width and balanced 3- or 3/4-thread stitch.** Serge-seam (Fig. 8-17). Test the seam by pulling; it should not pull away from the fabric.

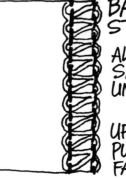

Fig. 8-17

For Durable Seams in Corduroy, Velveteen, and Velvet

(Fig. 8-18)

Fig. 8-18

1. **Serge-finish the edges with a wide, medium- to long-length, and balanced 3- or 3/4-thread stitch.** The serger will neatly finish the edges of pile fabrics. **Serge-finish raw edges of major garment seams** just after cutting

(Fig. 8-19). This will prevent raveling during construction. Be careful only to skim (not trim) the edges so that you can accurately gauge seam width later. **It is always easier to serge-finish seams before straight-stitching.**

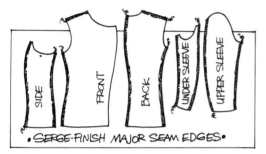

Fig. 8-19

2. **Straight-stitch the seam with a 5/8" seam allowance.**

For Decorative Seams That Will Have Little Stress

• **Adjust the serger for a wide, medium-length (3mm) and balanced 3- or 3/4-thread stitch.** Test on two layers of the fabric to see if the seam will pull away from the fabric. If it does, lengthen the stitch slightly.

• For decorative serging on the outside of the garment, **serge-seam with the wrong sides together.**

• For a less shiny finish, use **woolly nylon thread in the loopers and serge with the wrong sides together.** Loosen the tensions to allow the thread to fluff out and fill in between stitches.

Fast Hems

For Corduroy, Velveteen, and Velvets

1. **Serge-finish hems and lightly press them to the wrong side.**

2. With velvet, **hand-stitch** hems in place (Fig. 8-20). With corduroy and velveteen, **blindstitch with your sewing machine** (Fig. 8-21). Test to make sure the presser foot does not leave an imprint on the right side.

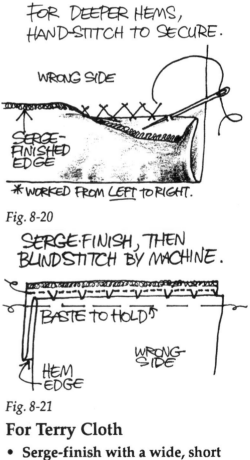

Fig. 8-20

Fig. 8-21

For Terry Cloth

• **Serge-finish with a wide, short (2.5mm) and balanced 3- or 3/4-thread**

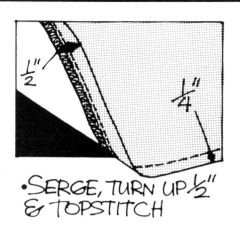

Fig. 8-22

stitch. Turn the hem allowance to the wrong side and topstitch (Fig. 8-22).

• **Serge-finish with *ThreadFuse* in the lower looper.** Turn to the wrong side and fuse in place.

• For variation, **use decorative thread in the upper looper and serge-finish from the wrong side.** Turn the hem allowance to the right side and edge-stitch (Fig. 8-23). Or use *ThreadFuse* in the lower looper and fuse the hem to the right side.

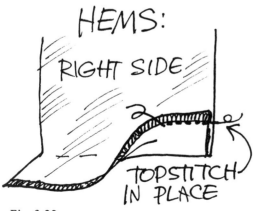

Fig. 8-23

Special Techniques

For setting sleeves into garments made of pile fabric, **sew in the sleeve with your sewing machine, then finish by serge-seaming the seam allowances together** (Fig. 8-24).

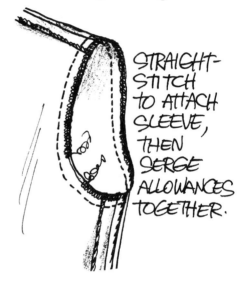

Fig. 8-24

Quick Tips

• For more accurate cutting, **trim the pattern pieces before laying them on the fabric.**

• **When sewing buttonholes, if the pile snags or pulls, place a piece of tissue paper under the fabric.** Tear away the tissue after stitching.

• When laundering pile fabrics, **turn the garment inside out to prevent snagging or pulling the pile.** This also prevents lint from clinging to the pile.

- Remove garments from the dryer while slightly damp and pull on the seamlines to straighten them and to prevent puckering.

- If the pile has flattened from wear, steam it well and **lightly fluff up the nap with a piece of self-fabric.** Or hang the garment in a steam-filled bathroom.

- **Use leftover pieces of velvet or velveteen to trim garments** made from other fabric. For example, make a soft and pretty collar and cuffs on a wool flannel dress.

Project: His-and-Hers Terry Coverup

(Fig. 8-25)

Fig. 8-25

For this quick coverup, you will need **3/4 yard of both 45"-wide cotton terry or terry velour and 3/4"-wide elastic,** enough to fit the waist or bust. (Use the velour for the right side of the fabric.)

✎ **Note:** If a 44" coverup will be too snug, purchase another 3/4 yard of fabric and cut two pieces of equal size to fit comfortably.

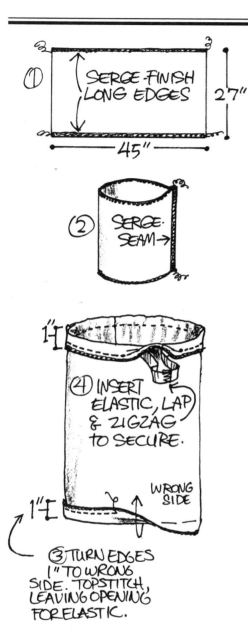

① SERGE-FINISH LONG EDGES

2'7"

45"

② SERGE-SEAM→

1"

④ INSERT ELASTIC, LAP & ZIGZAG TO SECURE.

WRONG SIDE

1"

③ TURN EDGES 1" TO WRONG SIDE. TOPSTITCH, LEAVING OPENING FOR ELASTIC.

Fig. 8-26

Pretreat the fabric. **Adjust the serger for the widest stitch, with a short length (2.5mm) and balanced 3- or 3/4-thread stitch.**

1. **Serge-finish both long edges** (Fig. 8-26).

2. **Serge-seam the 27" ends,** right sides together.

3. **Press 1" to the wrong side on both the upper and lower edges. Topstitch the hems in place,** leaving an opening in the upper hem to insert the elastic.

4. Thread the elastic through the upper hem and **secure it after fitting by lapping 1/2" and zigzagging.**

5. **Topstitch the opening closed.**

For variation, **thread the upper looper with decorative or contrasting thread.** Adjust the serger to a short stitch length. From the wrong side of the fabric, serge-finish both long edges. Turn the hems to the **right side** and edge-stitch to secure them.

9. Suedes, Leathers, and Synthetics Made Easy

Leathers, suedes, and the newer synthetics add luxury to any wardrobe. Sewing these fashionable, beautiful fabrics is easier than ever with serge-seaming and decorative serging. Serging is not necessary to finish the edges of leather but it helps to prevent slippage when seaming.

Fabric Choices

The uniformity of leathers and suedes vary greatly from skin to skin and also within the same skin. Leathers and suedes are sold by the square foot rather than by the yard.

Leather

• **Leather is the smooth outside of a skin.** Durable leathers are softer and more pliable than ever, thanks to the modern processes of splitting, dyeing, and finishing.

Suedes

• **Suedes are the inner side of the skin,** which is napped by a special brushing process.

Synthetic suedes and leathers look like real skins but are man-made, easy-care fabrics that are machine washable or dry-cleanable. These synthetic fabrics are also water-repellent and wrinkle-free.

Pattern Selection

Helpful Hints

• For pattern ideas, look at ready-to-wear's leather and leather-trimmed designs.

• **Select a simple design** with few seams for your first project.

• Many pattern companies feature patterns designed for leathers or synthetics.

• **The size of the piece of leather or suede may determine the design.** Almost everything made in leather will have to be pieced because of the various sizes of most skins (Fig. 9-1).

Fig. 9-1

- **For heavier skins, choose a tailored design** with little drape and detail.

- **The more body-conforming the style, the more supple the leather or synthetic should be.** Use lightweight leathers and suedes for pants and skirts. Supple leathers also drape beautifully (Fig. 9-2).

TOP: LIGHT-
WEIGHT
CHAMOIS;

PANTS:
CABRETTA

Fig. 9-2

- Synthetic leathers and suedes stretch in both the lengthwise and crosswise directions. **Use them with patterns designed for fabrics that have a small amount of ease.**

Calculate the Square Footage Required

Leather is sold by the square foot,
not by the yard. It's easy to convert yardage:

> One yard of 45" fabric =11 square feet of leather

> One yard of 54" fabric =13 square feet of leather

> One yard of 60" fabric =15 square feet of leather

Multiply the yardage requirement by the appropriate number of square feet, then add 15-20% for skin irregularities. Because dye lots vary, buy some extra leather for your project. Leftover leather is perfect for trim, yoke accents, belts, and fasteners.

Timesaving Notions

✎ **Note:** For more notions information, refer to the general Timesaving Notions section in the Introduction and the Notions Guidelines for Specialty Fabrics chart on page *x*. Notions with fabric-specific explanations are explained here.

- **Scissors or a rotary cutter and mat**

- **Pattern weights**

- **Machine needles**—Reserve triangular-pointed leather needles for thicker leathers.

- **Pins**

- **All-purpose or serger thread**

- **Buttonhole twist, pearl cotton or pearl rayon**

- *ThreadFuse*

- Woolly stretch nylon
- Marking pen

Interfacing

For Leathers and Suedes

Use nonfusible interfacing for natural leathers. Secure the interfacing in the seam allowances with a light layer of rubber cement (Fig. 9-3). Test various interfacing weights and types before applying cement to the garment pieces.

GLUING IN PLACE IN SEAM ALLOWANCES.

Fig. 9-3

For Synthetic Suede and Leather

Fusible woven or nonwoven interfacing works well with synthetics. To apply, use a damp press cloth on the wrong side of the fabric and steam generously with an iron at the wool setting.

Lining

Select a lining fabric that has the same care requirements as the outer fabric.

- Pants and jackets slide on and off more easily when they are lined.

- Lining prevents the garment from bagging out at the knees and elbows.

Fabric Preparation

Leathers and Suedes

No pretreating is necessary, but special care is required for cleaning most leathers and suedes. Skins pick up oil and grease easily and must be cleaned by a special process. (Solvents used in the ordinary dry-cleaning process will stiffen leathers and suedes.)

Synthetic Suede

Synthetic suede does not have to be preshrunk, but **pretreating will make the fabric softer and will help eliminate skipped stitches when serging or sewing.**

Synthetic Leather

This fabric shrinks up to 1/2" per yard in both width and length, so it must be pretreated. Machine wash it in warm water with a mild detergent. Tumble dry on low heat.

Pattern Layout and Cutting

- **Plan the layout and cut carefully.** If possible, lay out the pattern on the fabric before buying it. This is a real bonus when trying to minimize costs.

- **Test and fit the pattern with a similar-weight fabric,** such as denim, before cutting out leathers or synthetics.

- **Lay out the fabric single-layer, being sure to flip the pattern for the right and left side.** Make copies of the patterns from tissue or butcher paper for easier layout and cutting.

• **Lay out pattern pieces in the same nap direction,** especially when working with suedes. The fabric appearance changes with varying nap directions. Cutting with the nap running up will give the garment a richer, darker appearance (good for suedes).

• **Determine the direction of the nap by running your hand over the fabric.** If it is difficult to see, wrap the fabric over your shoulders and determine the nap direction by noting the difference in the fabric color.

When the fabric feels rough, the nap is running up and the color will appear darker and richer. **When the fabric feels smooth, the nap is running down** and the fabric will appear lighter in color and shinier.

• **With chalk, mark the nap direction on the back side of the fabric, close to selvage edge.** This ensures that all pieces will be cut in the same direction (Fig. 9-4).

• **Synthetic leather has no nap, so patterns can be laid in any direction if**

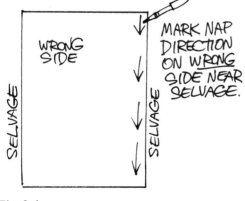

Fig. 9-4

stretch is not needed. When using a pattern designed for knits, lay it out with the greatest fabric stretch going around the body.

• **Use weights instead of pins** to avoid marring the fabric.

Tips for Real Leathers and Suedes

• Leather from the back and sides of an animal is better quality than that from the belly and legs.

• The lengthwise "grainline" is the animal's backbone (Fig. 9-5)

• Cut pieces that will endure the most

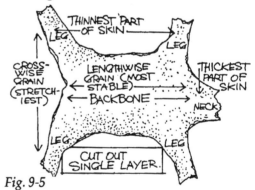

Fig. 9-5

stress from the center of a skin. This is the most stable part of the leather.

• Place pattern pieces directionally, with the top of each piece toward the top of the skin and the bottom of each piece toward the tail.

Pressing

Leathers may be pressed with low heat and no steam. Always press carefully from the wrong side. Test on scraps before pressing the garment.

Synthetics may be pressed with low heat and a press cloth. Do not touch the iron directly to the synthetic fabric, and press only from the wrong side of the garment.

Seams and Seam Finishes

Both conventional and flat seam methods work well with leathers and synthetics. Because the seams are difficult to press flat, **they are usually finished by topstitching, fusing, or gluing.** Both leathers and synthetics have a tendency to feed unevenly, but the serger helps solve this problem.

Seaming Tips

• **Do all fitting before stitching leathers or synthetics.** Ripping out seams can damage the fabric.

• **Pin inside the seam allowances,** making sure to remove any pins before they reach the knives (Fig. 9-6).

• **Use a medium-length 3-thread stitch (3.5mm) and loosen the tensions slightly** to prevent puckering.

• **Use taut sewing by holding both** layers of fabric taut in front of and behind the needle without pulling.

• For heavier fabrics, **reinforce serged seams with straight-stitching.** This is usually necessary for durability.

• When topstitching parallel rows, **stitch all the rows in the same direction to avoid pulling the fabric** (Fig. 9-7).

• **Edge-stitch,** rather than topstitching at 1/4", **to eliminate pulling the fabric.**

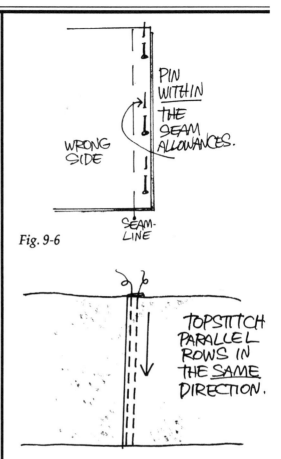

Fig. 9-6

Fig. 9-7

Inside Seaming of Leathers and Synthetics

• **Serge-seam with right sides together. Lightly press the seam to one side and, from the right side, edge-stitch close to the seamline** (Fig. 9-8). Or, using *ThreadFuse* in the lower looper, serge-seam and fuse the seam allowance to one side. Then edge-stitch to secure.

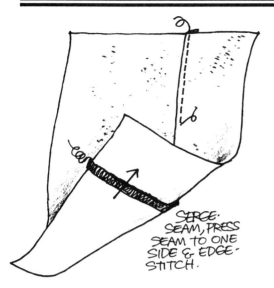

Fig. 9-8

• **Serge-finish the fabric edges, trimming 3/8". Straight-stitch a 1/4" seam and finger-press the seam open.** Edge-stitch on both sides of the seamline to secure (Fig. 9-9). Or use *Thread-Fuse* in the lower looper and carefully fuse the seam allowances open. Then edge-stitch to secure.

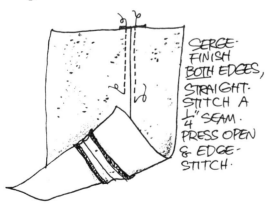

Fig. 9-9

• **Serge-finish the fabric edges, straight-stitch with a 5/8" seam allowance, and finger-press the seams**

open. Topstitch 1/4" on either side of the seamline to secure (Fig. 9-10). For leathers, **apply a narrow line of rubber cement under the seam allowance after stitching the seam.** Finger-press the seam open as the cement becomes tacky. Flatten by pressing with a pressing block. Topstitch when the cement is dry.

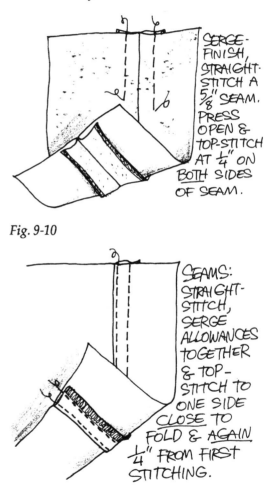

Fig. 9-10

Fig. 9-11

• **For a mock flat-felled seam (Fig. 9-11), straight-stitch with a 5/8" seam allowance. Using a wide, medium-length** and balanced 3- or 3/4-thread stitch, **serge the seam allowances together,** stitching close to the seamline and trimming as you serge. Press the seam allowances to one side. From the right side, **topstitch** close to the fold and, again, 1/4" from the first stitching. Another option is to **use** *ThreadFuse* **in the lower looper.** After serging the seam allowances together, press them to one side and fuse them in place. Topstitch with two rows of stitching, as shown in Fig. 9-11.

Decorative Serged Seams on the Outside of a Garment

• When the serged seam is on the outside of a garment, **your stitching must be top-quality and tensions must be set accurately.** To prevent uneven stitches, nothing should interfere with the even feeding of the looper threads (Fig. 9-12).

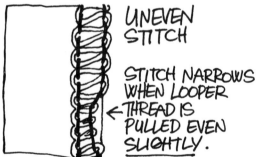

Fig. 9-12

• **For decorative outside seams,** thread the serger with decorative or contrasting thread in the upper looper and all-purpose or serger thread in the needle and lower looper. *ThreadFuse* also may be used in the lower looper.

Method 1
For Decoratively Serged Seams

Using a wide, short and balanced 3- or 3/4-thread stitch. Serge-seam with the wrong sides together, trimming the seam allowance. Press the seam to one side and edge-stitch (Fig. 9-13). Press all seams toward the back for consistency.

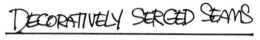

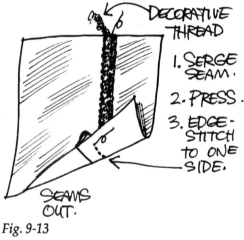

Fig. 9-13

Method 2
For Decorative Lapped Seams

Serge-finish the seamline edge of the top layer, with the right side up. Overlap the edges, matching the seamlines. Lap and edge-stitch, then topstitch, as shown (Fig. 9-14). From the wrong side, trim the under layer close to the stitching. Another option is to **use** *ThreadFuse* **in the lower looper** when serging the top layer. Fuse the seam to the bottom layer, then edge and topstitch.

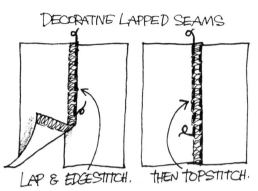

DECORATIVE LAPPED SEAMS

LAP & EDGESTITCH.   THEN TOPSTITCH.

Fig. 9-14

Edge Finishing

Serged Binding

Make a simple decorative-edge finish by serge-finishing the cut edge with a narrow balanced stitch. Or, for lighter-weight leathers and suedes, use a rolled edge (Fig. 9-15).

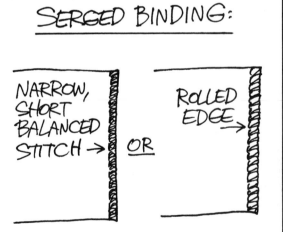

SERGED BINDING:

NARROW, SHORT BALANCED STITCH →   OR   ROLLED EDGE →

Fig. 9-15

1. On balanced-edge finishing, **thread both loopers with woolly stretch**

nylon thread for best coverage. For a rolled edge, use all-purpose or serger thread or decorative thread.

2. Adjust for a narrow, short and balanced 3-thread stitch. Serge-finish the cut edges. Test first on scraps of fabric. If the stitch is too short, the fabric will ripple and won't feed easily. **For rolled-edge finishing,** adjust the serger for a rolled edge and a long stitch. If the fabric does not roll easily, you may have to change the knife setting to a wider bite.

Faux-Braid Finishing
(Fig. 9-16)

Fig. 9-16

This finish is perfect for leather fabrics. Before serging the garment, always test and refine the finishing technique on scraps of fabric.

1. **Lightly press 3/8" to 1/2" toward the wrong side.** (Refer to Fig. 7-12, page 119.)

2. Using a long stitch (8 stitches/inch), **topstitch 1/8" from the fold.**

3. Thread the serger with decorative thread in the upper looper and adjust for a narrow, medium-length (2.5 to 3mm) and balanced 3-thread stitch. From the right side, **serge slowly over the folded edge,** being careful not to cut the fold.

4. On the wrong side, **trim the excess fabric close to the serging.**

Faux-Braid Special Tips

Follow Steps 1, 2, and 3 above. In Step 3, while serging over the fold, serge over two or three strands of filler cord, such as topstitching thread or crochet thread. **Position the filler cord over the front and under the back of the foot** and between the knife and the needle.

• **Pull on the filler cord to ease in the serged edge.** This is especially helpful when serge-finishing a curve.

• When finished, **weave the filler-cord tails under the serger stitches,** using a tapestry needle or loop turner.

Threadfused Faux-Braid

To allow for varied techniques, leave at least 1" seam allowances along the edges that will be trimmed with faux-braid (see Variations, on this page). Trim any excess seam allowances as you serge-finish.

1. Thread the serger with **decorative thread in the upper looper and** *ThreadFuse* **in the lower looper.** Use all-purpose or serger thread in the

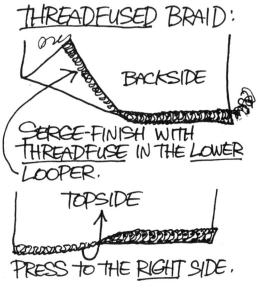

Fig. 9-17

needle (Fig. 9-17).

2. From the wrong side, **serge-finish the edge with a narrow, medium-length and balanced stitch.**

3. **Press carefully to the right side and fuse.**

4. Rethread and readjust the serger, **changing to all-purpose, serger, or decorative thread in the lower looper.** Adjust for a wide, medium-length stitch.

5. From the right side, **serge over the narrow balanced stitch.** The second layer makes it look more braid-like.

Variations: Follow Step 1 above. From the wrong side, serge-finish the edge with a wide, medium-length and balanced stitch. Then simply press the edge to the right side and fuse in place. To vary the look, vary the width of the fabric pressed to the right side, as shown (Fig. 9-18). (The narrower the seam allowance, the smoother it will turn along curved edges. Wider allowances are best for straighter edges.)

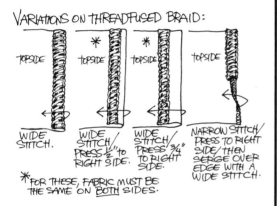

Fig. 9-18

Fast Hems

Avoid pinning the hem since pins may damage the fabric. Instead, fold the hem to the wrong side and hold it in place with large paper clips (Fig. 9-19).

Fig. 9-19

For easiest hemming of leathers, try one of the following methods:

• Serge-finish the edge and turn 5/8" to the wrong side. **Topstitch close to the fold and again 1/4" from the first stitching.**

• Or **serge-finish the edge using** *ThreadFuse* **in the lower looper.** Then turn 5/8" to the wrong side, fuse into position, and topstitch.

• **For leathers and suedes, serge-finish the hem and glue it into position with a thin layer of rubber cement.** A serge-finished edge will add durability to a glued hem.

Quick Tips

• When topstitching two rows 1/4" apart on skins or synthetics, **topstitch the row closest to the seam or folded edge first.** This will help prevent pulling between the stitched rows.

• **Use a long stitch length (8 stitches/inch) for edge- or topstitching.**

• **Fusing (with** *ThreadFuse***) or gluing the seam allowances in place helps prevent the fabric from pulling when edge- or topstitching.**

• When pressing any real or synthetic suede, **press over a terry towel to prevent flattening the nap.** Also, use a terry towel when applying fusible interfacing to synthetic suedes.

• **Set the differential feed to 2.0 to prevent stretching the leather.**

Fig. 9-20

Project: Quick-and-Easy Portfolio

(Fig. 9-20)

Materials Needed

• Pieces of leather or suede with the measurements shown in Fig. 9-21 or 5/8 yard of synthetic

• One spool of decorative or contrasting thread for binding the flap edge

• Two buttons with shanks

• One 15" leather, suede or synthetic lacing

1. **Cut one of both the portfolio and the flap facing using the measurements shown** (Fig. 9-21). For a stiffer, lined portfolio, fuse the entire square with light- to medium-weight, stable, nonwoven interfacing or fusible tricot.

2. Using decorative thread in the upper looper and a narrow, short and balanced stitch, **serge-finish the two 12" sides of the flap facing** (Fig. 9-22). *ThreadFuse* may be used in the lower looper for ease in binding. Weave the thread ends back through the underside of the serged edge.

3. With wrong sides together, **place the flap facing to one corner of the portfolio. The facing should extend about 1" beyond the corner of the portfolio** (Fig. 9-22). Fuse the facing in place using fusible web for synthetic fabrics or rubber cement for real leather.

4. Fold the 1" extension over the corner, just lapping the portfolio 1/4" (Fig. 9-23). (If using *ThreadFuse*, fuse in place.) **Edge-stitch to secure.**

5. Fold the portfolio right sides together at the midpoint between A and B on one side (Fig. 9-23). Using a wide stitch, **serge a 1/2" seam, trimming approximately 1/4".** Repeat for the other side labeled B and A.

6. Turn right side out and **apply the button fasteners. Tie on a leather or synthetic lacing** to wrap the buttons, manila-envelope style, and hold the portfolio flap closed (see finished view, Fig. 9-20).

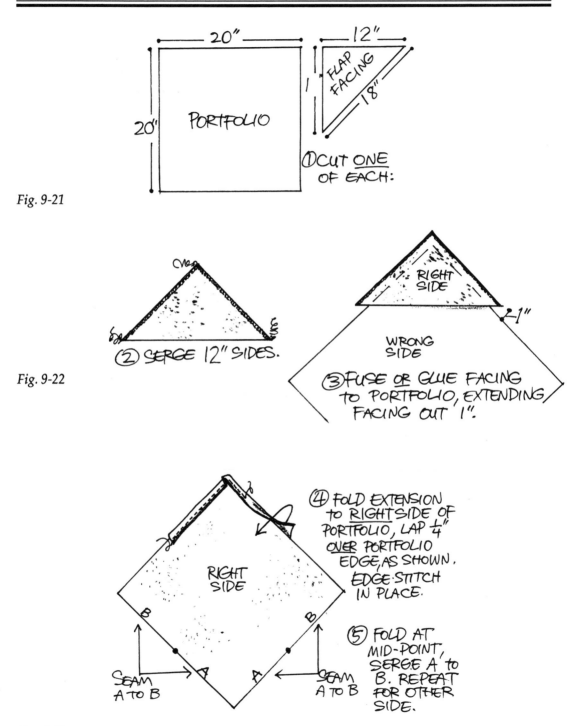

Fig. 9-21

20"

20"

PORTFOLIO

12"

FLAP FACING

18"

① CUT ONE OF EACH:

Fig. 9-22

② SERGE 12" SIDES.

RIGHT SIDE

WRONG SIDE

1"

③ FUSE OR GLUE FACING TO PORTFOLIO, EXTENDING FACING OUT 1".

RIGHT SIDE

④ FOLD EXTENSION TO RIGHT SIDE OF PORTFOLIO, LAP ¼" OVER PORTFOLIO EDGE, AS SHOWN. EDGE·STITCH IN PLACE.

⑤ FOLD AT MID-POINT, SERGE A to B. REPEAT FOR OTHER SIDE.

B   B

A   A

SEAM A TO B   SEAM A TO B

Fig. 9-23

10. *Fabulous Fake Furs*

Faux (fake) furs can provide the same luxury, beauty and warmth as the real thing and have several added advantages: easy care, added durability, and lower prices. With serging, constructing fake furs is quick and easy.

Fabric Choices

• High-quality faux furs have a soft, dense pile. They are available in many patterns and colors.

• Faux furs are made from acrylic or polyester and are usually machine-washable. **The pile is on the right side of the fabric, and most have a knit backing.**

Faux furs may be pelted or unpelted (Fig. 10-1). Matching seams is not required for unpelted "furs." However, seams in pelted "furs" can be easily disguised. Low and looped "furs" are the easiest to stitch, especially when seaming three or more thicknesses. For a first project, choose a light- to medium-weight faux fur.

Fig. 10-1

Pattern Selection

• When making a faux fur coat or jacket, **select a loose-fitting pattern with minimal seams and a simple collar and lapel.** A mandarin, un-notched collar or a boa-style collar are recommended.

• **Avoid patterns with darts, gathers, and pleats. The bulkiness of the pile makes these details difficult to stitch.**

• **Corresponding straight seams on pattern pieces can be overlapped and eliminated.** Use an extended facing instead of a sew-on facing to reduce the bulk of a seam (Fig. 10-2).

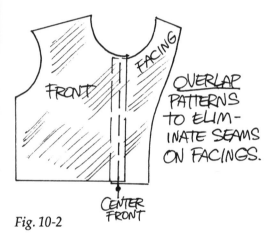

Fig. 10-2

• **Faux furs can also be used for collars, cuffs, hats, and linings** (Fig. 10-3).

• **If a pattern calls for buttonhole closures, use hooks and eyes or snaps instead.**

"FURS" USED FOR COLLARS, CUFFS & HATS.

Fig. 10-3

Timesaving Notions

✎ **Note:** For more notions information, refer to the general Timesaving Notions section in the Introduction and the Notions Guidelines for Specialty Fabrics chart on page *x*. Notions with fabric-specific explanations are explained here.

• **Scissors, rotary cutter or single-edged razor blade and mat**

• **Pattern weights**

• **Machine needles**

• **Pins**

• **All-purpose or serger thread**

• **Woolly stretch nylon**

• **Marking pen**

Interfacing

Interfacing is not necessary with fake furs.

Lining

Select a good-quality lining fabric that is heavy enough to be durable. Be sure it has the same care requirements as the "fur." Faux furs are much more comfortable to wear when lined.

Fabric Preparation

Most faux furs are machine-washable. **Pretreat faux furs to soften the backing and to fluff up the pile.** A softer backing makes the garment easier to serge.

Pattern Layout and Cutting

Cut the garment out using the "with nap" layout in the pattern cutting directions:

• **Determine the direction of the pile by running your hand over the fabric.** If it is difficult to determine the direction, wrap the fabric over your shoulders and determine the direction by comparing the difference in color. The side with the darker color has the pile running up; the side with the lighter color has the pile running down.

• **Cut the fabric with the pile running down the garment.**

• **With chalk, mark the direction of**

the pile on the back side of the fabric, close to the selvage, so you can be sure to cut all pieces in the same direction (Fig. 10-4).

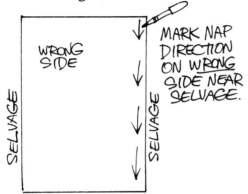

Fig. 10-4

• On pelted "fur," **the pelt lines must parallel the straight of grain.** Cut out and match as if the pelt lines formed an obvious stripe (Fig. 10-5).

• **Although you will cut the pattern pieces single-layer from the wrong side of the fabric,** determine where to position the pelt lines on the pattern by laying each pattern piece on the right side of the fabric. **Center a pelt line down the center back of the garment,** along the facing foldline, and down the center of the sleeves. Mark on the pattern where the pelt lines fall. **Flip the pattern pieces to mark the pelt lines on the right and left sides.** Try to arrange seamlines along pelt lines for less bulky seaming later. Position the other pattern pieces, incorporating as many full-width pelt sections as possible.

• **Mark the pelt lines on the wrong side of the fabric by pushing long pins through from the right side every 10" or so.** Then use a soap sliver or

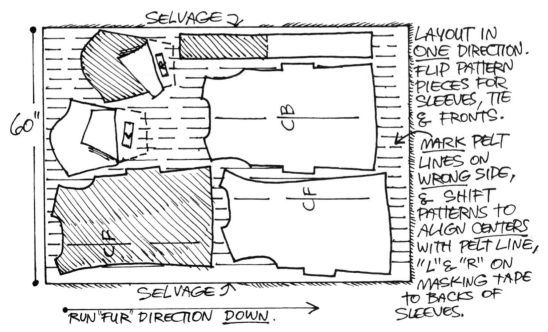

Fig. 10-5

dressmaker's chalk and a yardstick to mark the pelt lines. Lay the pattern pieces on the wrong side of the fabric, aligning the lengthwise grainlines with the pelt lines.

• **Cut side seam pockets from lining fabric to eliminate bulk.**

• When cutting the faux fur, cut through the backing only with the tips of sharp shears or a single-edge razor blade. Shorter, looped "furs" may be cut with a rotary cutter.

Pressing

Faux furs need no pressing. The pile can be fluffed by air-drying in the dryer.

Seams and Seam Finishes

When seaming, the upper layer of fabric has a tendency to slip and feed unevenly. The longer feed dogs of the serger will eliminate some of this fabric shifting.

Seaming Tips

• **Reduce the pressure on the presser foot to about half the normal setting.** The lighter pressure will eliminate flattening the pile. Lighter pressure will also allow the fabric to feed more easily.

• **Loosen the tensions** to serge this bulky fabric.

• **Sew in the direction of the pile** when serging in the lengthwise direction.

• **When straight-stitching seams, serge-finish the edges before seaming.** The serging flattens the edge for easier seaming and neatly finishes the cut edge. This prevents the fur from shedding during construction.

• With right sides together, **serge-seam the fabric with a medium- to wide-width, medium-length and balanced 3- or 3/4-thread stitch.**

• **Pin the seams parallel to and about 1" from the cut edges** (Fig. 10-6).

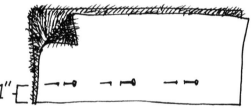

PIN PARALLEL TO CUT EDGES.

Fig. 10-6

• **Use taut seaming** by holding both layers of fabric taut in front of and behind the needle. Do this without pulling the fabric. From the right side, gently brush the nap with a fingernail brush or use a doll needle to pull the fur through the stitches and hide the seam.

Flatlock Seaming

Flatlock the seams of faux fur to eliminate bulk in the seamline. This seaming imitates the hinged seams used by furriers.

1. **Adjust for a narrow, long (4 to 5mm) 3-thread flatlock stitch.** The needle thread should be very loose; the upper looper thread, moderately loose; and the lower looper thread, tight.

2. Place the pieces right sides together. Using your serger tweezers, **brush the pile away from the cut edges, back between the layers of fabric.** This will make serging the heavy pile easier. **Flatlock the seam, trimming 3/8"** (Fig. 10-7).

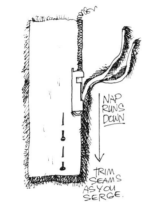

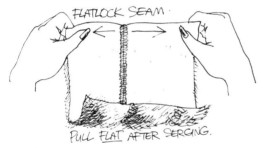

Fig. 10-7

3. **Pull the seam flat.** From the right side, gently brush the nap with a fingernail brush or use a doll needle to **pull the fur through the stitches** and hide the seam.

Flatlocking Tips

• For short-haired fur, **pretrim the seam allowances, then flatlock with a wide stitch.** Allow the stitches to hang halfway over the edge so the seam will pull completely flat.

• For lightweight fake furs with a shallow pile, use either a straight-stitched or serged seam. **Sleeves are serge-finished and sewn into the armholes with a straight-stitched seam.**

Edge Finishing

The serger finishes the edge of the "fur" fabric and prevents the pile from shedding.

Fast Hems

The hemming technique you choose will depend on the weight and bulk of the fabric.

• **For most faux furs, simply serge-finish the cut edge** with a wide, medium-length and balanced 3-thread stitch. **Turn the hem allowance (no more than 2-1/2") to the wrong side and hand-stitch** to secure. Trim away the facing where it meets the hem, as shown (Fig. 10-8).

Fig. 10-8

• **With heavier fake fur,** you may have to face the hem (Fig. 10-9). Here's how:

1. **Trim the hem allowance to 1-1/4".**

2. **Cut a bias facing strip of lightweight lining fabric.** It should be 3"

FACING A "FUR" HEM:

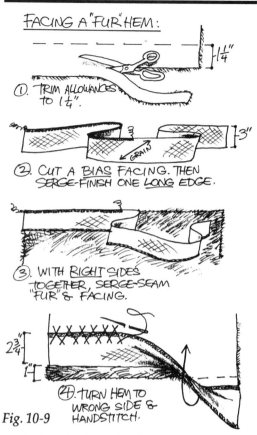

① TRIM ALLOWANCES TO 1¼".

② CUT A BIAS FACING. THEN SERGE-FINISH ONE LONG EDGE.

③ WITH RIGHT SIDES TOGETHER, SERGE-SEAM "FUR" & FACING.

④ TURN HEM TO WRONG SIDE & HANDSTITCH.

Fig. 10-9

wide by the length of the hem edge. Piece the strip if necessary. **Serge-finish one long edge of the strip** with a medium-width, balanced 3-thread stitch.

3. With right sides together, **match the cut edge of the "fur" to the unfinished edge of the facing strip.** Using the widest-width, balanced 3- or 3/4-thread stitch, **serge-seam the edges.**

4. **Turn the hem to the wrong side and hand-stitch to secure.**

Quick Tips

• When seaming smooth fabric to faux fur, **stitch in the direction of the "fur"**

nap with the smooth fabric on top.

• **Clean your serger often when sewing with faux furs.** They shed profusely, leaving lots of fuzz in machine parts.

Project: Quick-and-Easy Faux-Tailed Scarf

(Fig. 10-10)

FAUX-TAILED SCARF.

Fig. 10-10

Materials needed

• 3/4 yard of heavy-weight knit fabric, such as sweatering or doubleknit

• 1/2 yard faux fur

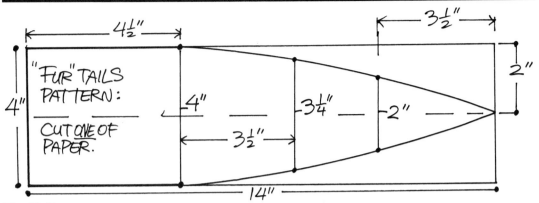

Fig. 10-11

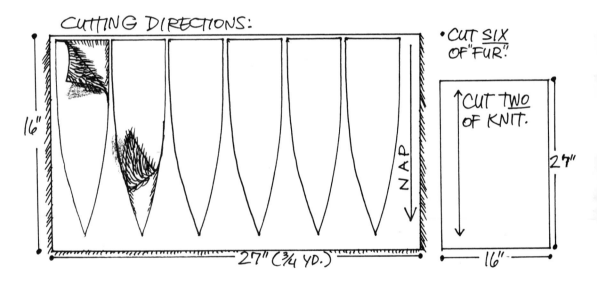

Fig. 10-12

1. Make the "fur" tails pattern as shown (Fig. 10-11). **Cut six pieces from the fabric with the nap running down** (Fig. 10-12). **Cut two 16" x 27" rectangles of the knit fabric.**

2. Adjust the serger for a wide, medium-length and balanced 3- or 3/4- thread stitch. With right sides together, fold the "fur" pieces in half lengthwise and serge-seam the long edges (Fig. 10-13). Stitch with the nap of the fabric, from the widest part to the point. Using a loop turner or crochet hook, **turn each tail right side out.**

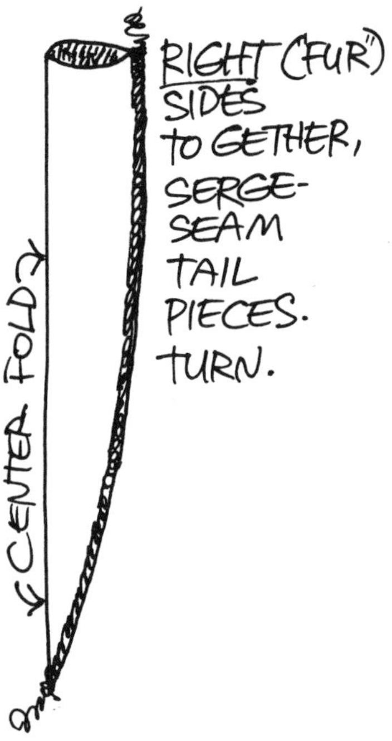

RIGHT ("FUR")
SIDES
TOGETHER,
SERGE-
SEAM
TAIL
PIECES.
TURN.

← CENTER FOLD →

Fig. 10-13

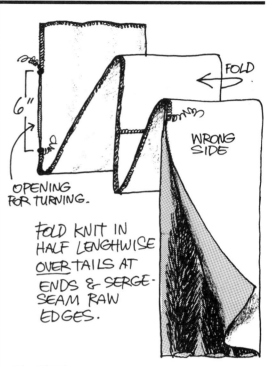

6"

OPENING
FOR TURNING.

FOLD KNIT IN
HALF LENGTHWISE
OVER TAILS AT
ENDS & SERGE-
SEAM RAW
EDGES.

FOLD

WRONG
SIDE

Fig. 10-14

3. With right sides together, **serge-seam the two pieces of knit fabric** together at one 16" end to make one long piece.

4. Fold the fabric in half lengthwise, with right sides together. Position the tails evenly inside (three at each end),

matching the cut edges. **Serge-seam the raw edges of the scarf,** catching the tails in the stitching and leaving a 6" opening on the side for turning (Fig. 10-14).

5. **Turn the scarf right-side out** and hand-tack the opening closed.

11. Special Tips for Quilted Fabrics and Vinyls

Serging Quilted Fabrics

QUILTED

• **When cutting** quilted fabrics, **do not compress the batting near the cut edges** (that means no pins, weights, or pressure from your hand). When the pressure is removed, the batting will pull in from the edge and distort the seamline.

• **When serging, be sure to catch the quilting threads in the stitching** at the edge of the fabric.

• When serging quilted fabrics, **first compress the layers with a wide, long zigzag stitch on your sewing machine and then serge.** Zigzagging will prevent the fabric from slipping and

forming pull lines when serged (Fig. 11-1). Serge, using the widest-width, medium-length and balanced 3- or 3/4-thread stitch.

COMPRESS LAYER(S) WITH ZIGZAGGING, THEN SERGE.

Fig. 11-1

• For a neat and easy edge finish, **serge the curved edges of a quilted project using a narrower-width serger stitch** (Fig. 11-2).

SERGE-FINISH CURVED EDGES WITH A NARROW STITCH WIDTH FOR A NEATER EDGE.

Fig. 11-2

Reversible-Edge Binding

To edge-finish a single layer of quilted fabric, use serged reversible-edge binding (Fig. 11-3).

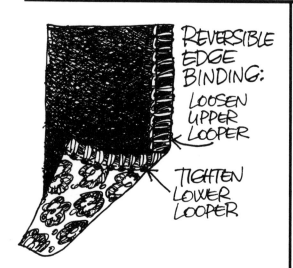

REVERSIBLE
EDGE
BINDING:

LOOSEN
UPPER
LOOPER

TIGHTEN
LOWER
LOOPER

Fig. 11-3

1. Thread heavier decorative thread in the upper looper.

2. Adjust for a narrow width and a short (2mm) stitch length.

3. Loosen the upper looper tension and tighten the lower looper tension **so the heavy thread wraps the edge.** If it does not wrap completely, narrow the stitch width or loosen the tension by removing the heavier thread from one of the thread guides or the tension dial.

Serging Vinyl Fabrics

• When serge-seaming vinyl, **adjust the serger for a medium- to wide-width, medium- to long-length and balanced 3-or 3/4-thread stitch.** A shorter stitch length may cause the vinyl to tear.

• **Use a sharp, fine needle,** size 11/75 or smaller, if available.

• Vinyl has a tendency to feed improperly on a sewing machine, but the long feed dogs of a serger help ensure an even feed. **Use taut sewing** by holding both layers of fabric taut in front of and behind the needle, without pulling the fabric through.

• **Lower the pressure on the presser foot** to allow easier feeding.

• Because pins and needles will leave permanent holes in vinyl, **fit the garment before stitching** to avoid having to rip out stitches. **Pin inside the seam allowances** and make sure to remove the pins before they reach the knives. Or hold the seam allowances together with paper clips.

• If the vinyl is heavy and the knives do not cut the fabric easily, **trim the seam allowances to 1/4" before serge-seaming.** Then either raise the knife or serge without trimming.

• **When topstitching, use a long stitch length** to avoid weakening or tearing the vinyl.

VINYL

Sources

Fabrics-by-Mail Directory

We recommend that every sewing enthusiast develop a special relationship with his or her local dealers and retailers for convenient advice and inspiration, plus the ease of coordinating purchases. However, when specialty items cannot be found locally or when a home sewer lives several miles from a sewing retailer, mail-order specialists are the best alternative.

☞ **Special Tip:** Chances are, nearby retailers will welcome your phone order. Just ask. If you're busy, it may allow you to shop locally without leaving the house.

The following list will make your search for these resources a breeze. Each company is listed under just one or two categories—the major product concentrations—although the company may offer other merchandise or services. *Our list is for reference only and does not carry our endorsement or guarantee.* (We have not knowingly included any questionable items or firms.) Enjoy.

☞ **Special Tip:** To streamline information gathering, be specific even when simply requesting samples or specific product brochures. Let the company know exactly what you are looking for—which may include color, fiber, texture, or size.

✎ **Note:** This was developed with permission from Gail Brown and Tammy Young's *Innovative Sewing*.

Risk-free Mail Order

• **Before you buy:** Read catalog descriptions carefully to make sure the product is what you want. Is there a guarantee? What is the policy for returns?

• **Placing your order:** Fill out the order form carefully and make a copy of both order and payment for future reference. Never send cash. When ordering by phone, complete the order form first to prevent mistakes. If possible, keep a record of the date of your phone order, as well as the name of the salesperson.

• **If there is a problem with your order:** Contact the company right away, by phone or by mail. If you contact by phone, be sure to record the time and date of your call, as well as the name of the contact person. Follow up in writing, describing the problem and outlining any solution reached during the phone call. Send copies of your order and payment record. Get a return receipt from the shipper when returning merchandise.

• **The "30-Day Rule":** If a delivery date isn't given in a company's materials, it must ship within 30 days of receiving your order (COD orders excepted), according to the Federal Trade Commission's Mail Order Merchandise Rule. If you place an order using a credit card, your account shouldn't be billed until shipment is made. If you send payment with your order and your order doesn't arrive when promised, you may cancel the order and get a full refund.

☞ **Special Tip**: In today's volatile business climate, any mail-order source list will change frequently. Please send your comments on any out-of-business notifications or unsatisfactory service to *Update Newsletters*, 2269 Chestnut, Suite 269, San Francisco, CA 94123.

Key to Abbreviations and Symbols:

SASE = Self-addressed, stamped (first class) envelope with your request.

L-SASE = Large SASE (2-oz. first-class postage) with your request.

(Check with your postmaster regarding Canadian mail.)

* = refundable with order.

= for information, brochure, or catalog.

Hard-to-Find Patterns and Designs

✎ **Note:** Patterns from the major companies (Butterick, McCall's, New Look, Simplicity, and Vogue) are readily available from your local fabric stores.

Campbell's, R.D.I. Box 1444, Herndon, PA 17830. Vintage-look patterns. $4#.

Fabric Fancies, 501 Evans Ave., Reno, NV 89512, 702/323-0117. Historic frontier garment patterns. $2#.

Ghee's, 106 E. Kings Highway, Suite 205, Shreveport, LA 71104, 318/868-1154. Patterns and notions for making handbags. $1#.

Great Copy Patterns, Stretch & Sew Fabrics, P.O. Box 85329, Racine, WI 53408, 414/632-2660. One-size-fits-all pattern styling for knits. L-SASE#.

Great Fit Patterns, 221 S.E. 197th, Portland, OR 97233, 503/665-3125. Fashionable styles created exclusively for the large figure, sizes 38-60. $1#.

Jean Hardy Patterns, 2151 La Cuesta Dr., Santa Ana, CA 92705. Patterns for riding, cheerleading, skating, and square dancing. $1#.

Kids Can Sew, P.O. Box 1710, St. George, UT 84771-1710, 800/I-MADE-IT. Patterns for kids' clothes, plus teach-kids-to-sew training materials. Free#.

Kwik-Sew Pattern Co., Inc., 3000 Washington Ave., N., Minneapolis, MN 55411, 612/521-7651. Kwik-Sew Patterns (Canada), Ltd., 5035 Timberlea Blvd., Unit #7, Mississauga, Ontario L4W 2W9 Canada, 416/625-0135. Easy-to-sew fashions for the whole family. Choose from 800 patterns. $3.50# ($4 in Canada).

Logan Kits, Route 3, Box 380, Double Springs, AL 35553, 205/486-7732. Lingerie and activewear kits for men, women, and children. $1 and L-SASE#.

Peg's Fabric and Yarn Closet, 4110 Callfield Road, Wichita Falls, TX 76308. Peg's Pieces patterns. SASE#.

Picks Fine Handwovens, 3316 Circle Hill Rd., Alexandria, VA 22305. Handwoven silk skirt lengths and matching sweater yarns packaged with lining, notions, and sewing/knitting instructions. Swatches, $2.

Pineapple Appeal, P.O. Box 197, Owatonna, MN 55060, 507/455-3041. Sweatshirts, jams, pillows, windsocks, and tote bags kits for the beginning sewer. Free#.

Prime Moves, P.O. Box 8022, Portland, OR 97207. Authentic aerobic wear. $1#.

Raindrops & Roses, 8 SE 199 Ave., Portland, OR 97233. Maternity and nursing wear patterns. $1#.

Richard the Thread, 8320 Melrose Ave., West Hollywood, CA 90069. Historic period patterns and notions. $2#.

Seams Sew Easy, P.O. Box 2189, Manasses, VA 22110. Swimwear patterns (two-piece). L-SASE#.

Serging Ahead, P.O. Box 45, Grandview, MO 64030. Knit patterns and supplies. $1#.

Stretch & Sew Inc., P.O. Box 185, Eugene, OR 97440. Multisized patterns for women, men, and children. Free#.

Sunrise Designs, Box 277, Orem, UT 84059. Infant, toddler, and children's patterns. Several easy-to-sew designs in each multisized pattern. Free#.

Susan's Sewing Center, 68-720 Highway 11, Cathedral City, CA 92234. *Patterns by the Yard.* L-SASE#.

U-Sew-Knits, P.O. Box 43078, Phoenix, AZ 85080. Precut women's sportswear and children's clothing kits. SASE#.

Yes Mam Lingerie & Fashions, P.O. Box 1822, Leesburg, FL 32749-1822. Kits for lingerie, men's lounge wear, and women's fashions. $1 and SASE#.

Embellishments

Badhir Trading, Inc., 8429 Sisson Hwy., Eden, NY 14057, 716/992-3193. Appliqués, bead/pearl fringe, sequins, and jewels for bridal and evening wear. $2*#.

Baubanbea Enterprises, Box 1205, Smithtown, NY 11787. Rhinestones, sequins, beads, jewels, lace, appliqués, feathers, silk flowers, fabrics, and more. $4#.

Collections, P.O. Box 806, Ithaca, NY 14851. Laces, 3/8" to 60" wide, including Rose Garden, Point d'esprit, lingerie, stretch and fiberfill lace. Free#.

Creative Trims, 18 Woodland Drive, Lincroft, NJ 07738. Lace, embroideries, and ribbons. Free#.

Donna Lee's Sewing Center, 25234 Pacific Hwy. S., Kent, WA 98032, 206/941-9466. Imported laces and Swiss embroideries; silk ribbons and French trims; Swiss batiste and China silks. $3#.

Elsie's Exquisiqués, 513 Broadway, Niles, MI 49120, 616/684-7034. French-reproduction laces, trims, silk ribbons, hand-crafted ribbon roses, and insertion laces.

Greatest Sew on Earth, P.O. Box 214, Fort Tilden, NY 11695. Sequin and jeweled trims and appliqués, eyelet embroideries, bridal laces, and pearls. $1#.

Lace Place, 9250 N. 43rd Ave., Ste. 6, Glendale, AZ 85302. Assorted laces. $2#.

Lace Plus, Inc., P.O. Box 3243, Fort Lee, NJ 07024. Fine quality Schiffli laces in a variety of widths and designs. $2# w/ swatches.

Lacis, 2982 Adeline, Berkeley, CA 94703. A multitude of new and antique laces. Also, lacemaking supplies and interesting needlework tools and notions. $1.50#

Pioneer Specialty Products, Box 412, Holden, MA 01520. Laces, ribbons, eyelet, tape. $1*#.

Notions Specialists

Aardvark Adventures, P.O. Box 2449, Livermore, CA 94551, 415/443-2687. Books, beads, buttons, bangles, plus unusual assortment of related products. Decorative thread, including metallics. $1#.

The Bee Lee Company, P.O. Box 36108-B, Dallas, TX 75235. Complete selection of threads, zippers, notions, and trims, including Western styles. Free#.

C. J. Enterprises, 2219 E. Thousand Oaks Blvd., Ste. 336, Thousand Oaks, CA 91362, 818/702-6029. Unique sewing machine feet for special applications, made to fit all makes and models. Ask for dealer referrals. L-SASE#.

Catherine's, Rt. 6, Box 1227, Lexington, NC 27292, 704/798-1595. Threads and more at wholesale prices. Minimum order, $35. School quantity discounts. $2 and L-SASE for thread color card.

Clotilde, Inc., 1909 SW First Ave., Ft. Lauderdale, FL 33315, 305/761-8655. Catalog of over 1,200 items, including special threads and notions, sewing tools, and supplies, books, and videos. $1#.

Custom Zips, P.O. Box 1200, So. Norwalk, CT 06856. Zippers cut to order. $2#.

D & E Distributing, 199 N. El Camino Real, Ste. F-242, Encinitas, CA 92024. Decorative threads and yarns, including silk, rayon, and Madeira metallics. L-SASE#.

The Embroidery Stop, 1042 Victory Dr., Yardley, PA 19067. Threads, yarns, needles. $2#.

Fit For You, 781 Golden Prados Dr., Diamond Bar, CA 91795, 714/861-5021. Sewing notions, accessories, videos, and square-dance patterns. L-SASE#.

Hemming's, 2645 White Bear Ave., Maplewood, MN 55109, 612/770-4130. Sewing machine accessories and furniture, professional pressing supplies, and a wide range of notions. Free#.

Home-Sew, Dept. S, Bethlehem, PA 18018. Basic notions, trims, coned threads, and tools. Free#.

Jacquart's, 505 E. McLeod, Ironwood, MI 49938, 906/932-1339. Zippers. $1#.

Madeira, 30 Bayside Court, P.O. Box 6068, Laconia, NH 03246. Decorative threads—from metallics and sequin strands, to trendy neons and rayons. $30 minimum. L-SASE#.

Maryland Trims, P.O. Box 3508, Silver Spring, MD 20901. Laces, sewing notions, and supplies. $1.75#.

Mill End Store, Box 02098, Portland, OR 97202, 503/236-1234. Broad selection of notions, trims, threads, and accessories. SASE#.

Nancy's Notions, Ltd., P.O. Box 683, Beaver Dam, WI 53916. Over 300 sewing notions and accessories, threads, and tools, interfacings and fabrics, books and videos. Free#.

National Thread & Supply, 695 Red Oak Rd., Stockbridge, GA 30281, 800/847-1001, ext. 1688; in GA, 404/389-9115. Name-brand sewing supplies and notions. Free#.

Newark Dressmaker Supply, P.O. Box 2448, Lehigh Valley, PA 18001, 215/837-7500. Sewing notions, trims, buttons, decorative threads, and supplies. Free#.

Oregon Tailor Supply Co., Inc., P.O. Box 42284, Portland, OR 97242, 800/678-2457 (orders only). Every kind of notion imaginable. L-SASE#.

The Paris Connection, 4314 Irene Dr., Erie, PA 16510. A wide variety of notions, feet, books, and patterns, including old sewing-machine manuals. $1.50#.

The Perfect Notion, 566 Hoyt St., Darien, CT 06820, 203/968-1257. Hard-to-find notions and threads (including their *ThreadFuse*™ melt adhesive thread). $1#.

Serge & Sew Notions, 11761 99th Ave. N., Maple Grove, MN 55369, 612/493-2449. Threads, books, patterns, furniture, fabrics, and more, priced 20-40% below retail. Free#. Swatch club, $6 for six months.

Serging Ahead, P.O. Box 45, Grandview, MO 64030. Threads, books, and patterns. $1#.

Sew-Art International, P.O. Box 550, Bountiful, UT 84010. Decorative threads, notions, and accessories. Free#.

SewCraft, P.O. Box 1869, Warsaw, IN 46580, 219/269-4046. Books, decorative threads, and notions.

Sew/Fit Co., P.O. Box 565, La Grange, IL 60525, 312/579-3222. Sewing notions and accessories; modular tables for serger/sewing machine setup; cutting tools and mats, books. Free#.

Sewing Emporium, 1087 Third Ave., Chula Vista, CA 92010, 619/420-3490. Hard-to-find sewing notions, sewing machine cabinets, and accessories. $2#.

The Sewing Place, 18870 Cox Ave., Saratoga, CA 95070. Sewing machine needles and feet, plus books by Gale Grigg Hazen. Specify your brand and model if ordering machine accessories. L-SASE#.

The Sewing Workshop, 2010 Balboa St., San Francisco, CA 94121, 415/221-SEWS. Unique designer notions and supplies. L-SASE#.

Solo Slide Fasteners, Inc., P.O. Box 528, Stoughton, MA 02072, 800/343-9670. All types and lengths of zippers, other selected notions. Free#.

Speed Stitch, 3113-D Broadpoint Dr., Harbor Heights, FL 33983. Machine art kits and supplies, including all-purpose, decorative, and specialty threads, books, and accessories. $3*#.

Thread Discount & Sales, 7105 S. Eastern, Bell Gardens, CA 90201, 213/562-3438. Coned polyester thread. SASE#.

Threads & Things, P.O. Box 83190, San Diego, CA 92138, 619/440-8760. 100% rayon thread. Free#.

Threads West, 422 E. State St., Redlands, CA 92373, 714/793-4405 or 0214. Coned thread, machine parts, and accessories. SASE for free thread color list.

Treadleart, 25834 Narbonne Ave., Ste. I, Lomita, CA 90717, 800/327-4222. Books, supplies, notions, decorative threads, and creative inspiration. $1.50#. Bimonthly color catalog/magazine, $12 annually.

T-Rific Products Co., P.O. Box 911, Winchester, OR 97495. Coned thread. Thread color chart, $1.25.

Two Brothers, 1602 Locust St., St. Louis, MO 63103. Zipper assortment. SASE#.

YLI Corporation, 45 W. 300 North, Provo, UT 84601, 800/854-1932 or 801/377-3900. Decorative, specialty, and all-purpose threads, yarns, and ribbons. $1.50#.

Sensational Silks

Fabric Fancies, P.O. Box 50807, Reno, NV 89513. White silks, satins, and jacquards for wedding gowns and lingerie. Imported laces, English illusion, and French net. $10# w/swatches.

Oriental Silk Co., 8377 Beverly Blvd., Los Angeles, CA 90048, 213/651-2323. Tussahs, chiffons, voiles, brocades, velvets, and more. Samples, $1*/for each fabric type specified.

Sureway Trading, 826 Pine Ave., Ste. 5, Niagara Falls, NY 14301, 716/282-4887. Silk fabrics and threads; silk/wool blends. Samples: naturals/whites, $8; colors, $12.

Thai Silks, 252 State St., Los Altos, CA 94022, 800/722- SILK; in CA, 800/221-SILK. Every type of silk imaginable. Fabric club, $10/year (three swatched mailings). Full swatch set (over 600), $20 ($18*).

Top Drawer Silks Ltd., 1938 Wildwood, Glendale Heights, IL 60139. Range of silk fabrications. Annual membership, $13# w/swatches.

Utex Trading, 710 Ninth St., Ste. 5, Niagara Falls, NY 14301, 416/596-7565. Silk fabrics, yarns, and threads. Complete sample set, $35*.

For Formals, Proms, and Weddings

Bridal-by-the-Yard, P.O. Box 2492, Springfield, OH 45501. Imported and domestic laces and fabrics. $7# w/ swatches.

Bridal Elegance, 1176 Northport Dr., Columbus, OH 43235. Bridal Elegance patterns, sizes 4-22, and Wedding Gown Design Book. $.50#.

Bridals International, 45 Albany St., Cazenovia, NY 13035. Imported laces and fabrics; button loops and covered buttons for wedding gowns. $7.50*#.

Fabric Fancies, 501 Evans Ave., Reno, NV, 89512, 702/323-0117. Complete line of wedding supplies. Lace catalogue, $10*. Bridal silks, $10*. Embroidered satin samples, $10*, and embroidered organza samples, $10* (both sets,

$16*). Bridal Elegance® Patterns brochure, $1. Wedding gown design book, $9. Historical bridal patterns brochure, $1. Also, books and videos.

La Sposa Veils, 252 W. 40th St., New York, NY 10018, 212/354-4729 or 944-9142. Bridal headpieces. $3*#.

Mylace, P.O. Box 13466, Tallahassee, FL 32317, 800/433-8859; in FL, 800/433-8857. Extensive selection of trim and French bridal laces from 1/4" to 50" wide. $3.50#.

Patty's Pincushion, Inc., at Grande Affaires, 710 Smithfield St., Pittsburgh, PA 15219, 412/765-3010. Fabrics for the bridal party plus personalized service for planning wedding gowns. Swatches available.

Sew Elegant, 15461 Dorian St., Sylmar, CA 91342. Custom wedding gown kits, containing fabrics, laces, notions, and multisized patterns. $5*# w/ swatches.

S-T-R-E-T-C-H & Knit Fabrics

ABC Knits, 13315 433rd Court, S.E., North Bend, WA 98045 Acrylic, cotton, and wool-blend knits; coordinated ribbing. L-SASE#.

Artknits by Clifford, 2174 Gary Rd., Traverse City, MI 49684, 616/943-8218. Custom-knit ribbing. SASE#.

Bead Different, 1627 S. Tejon, Colorado Springs, CO 80906, 303/473-2188. Stretch fabrics for dancers, skaters, and gymnasts. Send SASE with inquiry.

Beth McLeod, 1113 87th St., Daly City, CA 94015, 415/992-8731. Cotton/ *Lycra*® and nylon/*Lycra*® stretch knits. $1 and SASE#.

Cottons Etc., 228 Genesee St., Oneida, NY 13421, 315/363-6834. Knits, sweatshirting, *Lycra®*, and more. L-SASE# w/swatches.

Everitt Knitting Co., 234 W. Florida St., Milwaukee, WI 53204. All types of sweater yardage, plus matching ribbing and trims. Write for retailer referrals.

Golden Needles, 2320 Sauber Ave., Rockford, IL 61103. Custom-knit sweater yardage, sweater bodies with knitted name, and ribbing. Free swatches.

Just Rite Fabrics, RR3, Box 83B, Norton, KS 67654. Interlocks with matching ribbing, wool knits, stretch terry, and more. L-SASE and $2# (swatches included).

Kieffer's Lingerie Fabrics & Supplies, 1625 Hennepin Ave., Minneapolis, MN 55403. Swimwear nylon/cotton *Lycra®* blend stretch knits, sweatshirting, lingerie tricot. Also, many coned threads at bargain prices. Free#.

LG Fashions and Fabrics, P.O. Box 58394, Renton, WA 98058. *Lycra®*-blend knits of cotton and nylon. $2*# w/swatches.

Marianne's Textile Products (formerly Diversified Products), Box 319, RD 2, Rockwood, PA 15557. Sweater bodies, ribbing, knit collars. $2 and L-SASE#.

Rosen & Chadick, 246 W. 40th St., New York, NY 10018. Cotton/*Lycra®* and nylon/*Lycra®* stretch knits. SASE#.

Sew Smart, P.O. Box 776, Longview, WA 98632. Ribbed knit collars, trims, and snaps. L-SASE#.

Stretch & Sew Fabrics, 1165 Valley River Dr., Eugene, OR 97401. Stretch & Sew patterns, plus a complete assortment of knit fabrics and notions. L-SASE#.

Stretch & Sew Fabrics, 19725 40th Ave. W., Lynnwood, WA 98036. A complete selection of knits, Stretch & Sew patterns, and related notions. L-SASE#.

The Thrifty Needle, 3232 Collins St., Philadelphia, PA 19134. Sweater bodies and ribbing. $2 and SASE# w/swatches.

Cycling, Hiking, Dancing, and Skiing Materials

Altra, Inc., 100 E. Washington St., New Richmond, IN 47967, 317/339-4653. Precut and pattern sportswear kits for outdoor activities, including skiing, backpacking, and cycling; skiwear fabrics and fleece; outerwear hardware and supplies. $1#.

DK Sports, Daisy Kingdom, 134 N.W. 8th, Portland, OR 97209, 503/222-9033. Kits and patterns for active sportswear and outerwear (skiing, bicycling, aerobics, swimwear, and rainwear). Outerwear fabrics, including *Taslan®*, mountain cloth, *Cordura®*, *Gore-tex®*, and vertical stretch ski pant fabric. $2#.

Donner Designs, Box 7217, Reno, NV 89510. Outerwear and activewear kits featuring water-repellent fabrics. Outerwear fabrics, including *Tasnylon*, one- and two-way stretch, and *Gore-tex®*. Teacher discounts. $1#.

Frostline Kits, 2512 W. Independent Ave., Grand Junction, CO 81505, 800-KITS USA. Fabrics and precut kits for sportswear, outdoor clothing, luggage, camping gear, and more. Free#.

Green Pepper, Inc., 941 Olive, Eugene, OR 97407, 503/345-6665. Active and outerwear patterns and fabrics, including nylon/*Lycra*® and polypropylene/*Lycra*® knits, water-repellent fabrics, and insulating battings. $2#.

The Rain Shed, 707 N.W. 11th, Corvallis, OR 97330. Large selection of outerwear fabrics, kits, sewing notions, and tools. $1#.

Sundown Kits, 23815 43rd Ave. So., Kent, WA 98032-2856. Kits for assorted outerwear. $1#.

Timberline Sewing Kits, Inc., Box 126-SUB, Pittsfield, NH 03263, 603/435-8888. Fabrics and kits for outerwear and gear. $1#.

Fake Furs

Amanda Scott Publishing, P.O. Box 40425, Cinncinnati, OH 45240, 513/851-8936. Fake-fur fabrics, patterns, and kits. Swatch set, $8#*.

Wardrobe Fabrics

Baer Fabrics, 515 E. Market St., Louisville, KY 40202, 800/288-2237; 502/583-5521. Comprehensive selection of fabrics. Seasonal sample sets (prices vary). Custom swatching available. Notions, $2#.

Britex-by-Mail, 146 Geary, San Francisco, CA 94108, 415/392-2910. Designer fabrics, including unusual sweater knits. Personalized swatching and special offerings. $3 and L-SASE#.

Camille Enterprises, P.O. Box 615-N, Rockaway, NJ 07866. Variety of fabrics,

from the usual to designer. Four swatch mailings a year, $3 each; $10* a set.

Carolina Mills Factory Outlet, Box V, Hwy. 76, West Branson, MO 65616, 417/334-2291. Designer fabrics from major sportswear manufacturers, 30-50% below regular retail. Sample swatches, $2.

Classic Cloth, 2508-D McMullen Booth Rd., Dept. UN, Clearwater, FL 34621, 813/799-0417. Austrian boiled wool, dyed-to-match wool trim, and coordinating paisley challis. Swatches, $5* a set.

Clearbrook Woolen Shop, P.O. Box 8, Clearbrook, VA 22624, 703/662-3442. Variety of fabrics, with emphasis on wool. 8-10 sample sets per year. Free swatched mailings—send name and address to be placed on the mailing list.

The Cloth Cupboard, P.O. Box 2263, Boise, ID 83701, 208/345-5567. Japanese woodblock prints. Swatches, $2.50 and SASE.

The Couture Touch, P.O. Box 681278, Dept. UN, Schaumburg, IL 60168, 312/310-8080. Famous-name fashion fabrics, including Anglo, Landau, and Logantex. Complimentary seasonal swatch collection available.

Creative Fabrics, 3303 Long Beach Rd., Oceanside, NY 11572. Fine wool and polyester suitings, silk and silky polyesters, and challis. Swatches, $5*; $7 Canadian.

Creative Line Fabric Club, 101 Tremont St., Boston, MA 02108, 617/426-1473. Exclusive Italian imports, all natural fibers: silks, wools, cashmere, linens. Annual membership $25 (Canada, $35)—three swatch collections.

Cy Rudnick's Fabrics, 2450 Grand, Kansas City, MO 64108, 816/842-7808. Extensive collection of designer and specialty fabrics. Swatching service available. $3*, plus your personal color and fabric request.

Designer's Touch, 7689 Lakeville Hwy., Petaluma, CA 94952, 707/778-8550. Imported and domestic designer fabrics offered through representatives nationwide. Fashion Club membership also available—$50/year for 9-10 mailings of swatched fashion portfolios.

Elegance Fabrics, 91A Scollard St., Toronto, Ontario M5R IG4, Canada, 416/966-3446. Finest European fabrics—wools, silks, linens, cottons. Seasonal swatch catalogs: 300-swatch edition, $60*; 460 swatches plus notions, $100*; 460 larger swatches plus notions, $150*.

Exquisite Fabrics, Inc. (formerly Watergate Fabrics), Dept. SUB, 1775 K St. NW, 1st Floor, Washington, DC 20006, 202/775-1818. Exclusive fabrics from France, Switzerland, and Italy: exquisite bridal fabrics and laces, silks, cashmeres, cottons, and worsted woolens. Complimentary swatching service.

The Fabric Club, P.O. Box 28126, Atlanta, GA 30358. Exclusive designer fabrics at a 50-75% savings. Annual membership, $8, for four coordinated fabric brochures.

Fabric Gallery, 146 W. Grand River, Williamston, MI 48895, 517/655-4573. Imported and domestic silks, wools,

cottons, and better synthetics. $5/year for four swatched mailings.

Fabrications Fabric Club, Box 2162, South Vineland, NJ 08360. Fabrics from designers, ready-to-wear manufacturers, and mills. Four mailings, $10/year ($5*).

Fabricland, Inc., Box 20235, Portland, OR 97220, 800/255-5412. Full bolts of fabric or boxes of notions available. Minimum order, $50. Write for price list.

Fabrics by Mail, 1252 Woodway Rd., Victoria, BC V9A 6Y6, Canada, 604/384-9573. Coordinated cottons, silks, wools, and synthetics. $5#(*2.50 refundable voucher).

Fabrics in Vogue, 200 Park Ave., Ste. 303 E., New York, NY 10166. Imported wools, silks, linens, cottons, and blends featured in Vogue Patterns. Six swatch mailings, $10/year.

Fabrics Unlimited, 5015 Columbia Pike, Arlington, VA 22204, 703/671-0324. Better fashion fabrics from designer cutting rooms.

Fashion Fabrics Club, 10490 Baur Blvd., St. Louis, MO 63132. Variety of quality designer and name-brand fabrics at moderate prices. Swatches monthly, $7/year.

Field's Fabrics, 1695 44th S.E., Grand Rapids, MI 49508, 616/455-4570. *Ultrasuede®, Facile®, Caress®,* and *Ultraleather®* swatches, $10; silk, *Pendleton®* wool, metallics, and more (write for swatch information).

Four Seasons Fabric Club, 811 E. 21st St., North Vancouver, BC V7J 1N8, Canada. Coordinated fabric selections identified by personal color season. $25/year for four swatch mailings.

G Street Fabrics, 11854 Rockville Pike, Rockville, MD 20852, 301/231-8998. Extensive selection of better fabrics. Over 20 basic fabric charts available, including cotton, wool, silk, *Ultrasuede®, Facile®* ($10 each). Sample subscription ($35/six months, $50/year) for 60 swatches per month. Custom sampling, $1/garment. Notions, $4#. Professional discounts.

Ginette's Haute Couture Fabrics, 36 Charles St., Milton, Ontario L9T 2G6, Canada. Cottons, linens, silks, denims, and easy-care blends at a savings of 20-50% off regular retail prices. Two catalogs, $15 Canadian/year.

Grasshopper Hill Fabrics, 224 Wellington St., Kingston, Ontario K7K 2Y8, Canada, 613/548-3889. Fine fabrics at competitive prices. Semi-annual catalog, $5 Canadian ($2.50*).

House of Laird, 521 Southland Dr., P.O. Box 23778, Lexington, KY 40523, 606/276-5258. Designer fabrics offered through fabric showings by representatives nationwide. Write or call for information.

Imaginations, P.O. Box 2749, Westport, CT 06880. Discounts on coordinated groupings of knits and wovens, many from top label cutting rooms. Yearly subscription, $10 (Canada, $15).

J. J. Products Ltd., 117 W. Ninth St., Ste. 111, Los Angeles, CA 90015, 213/624-1840. Imported wool at discount prices. Swatch cards, $3* each.

Jehlor Fantasy Fabrics, 730 Andover Park W., Seattle, WA 98188, 206/575-8250. Variety of stretch fabrics, $2.50#. *Baubles, Bangles and Beads* catalog, $2.50. Ballroom dance costume patterns—SASE#.

Katsuri Dyeworks, 1959 Shattuck Ave., Berkeley, CA 94701, 415/841-4509. Fabrics from Japan. $5*#.

Left Bank Fabric Co. by Mail, 8354 W. Third St., Los Angeles, CA 90048, 213/655-7289. European silks, wools, cottons. Membership, $25*/year, for three collections.

The Material World, 5700 Monroe St., Sylvania, OH 43560, 419/885-5416. Imported and domestic silks, wools, and cottons. Quarterly swatch collections, $6/year.

Maxine Fabrics, 62 W. 39th St., Ste. 902, New York, NY 10018, 212/391-2282. Moygashel linens and blends, Liberty prints, *Ultrasuede®* and *Facile®*, coordinated silks, cottons, and novelties. $3# w/swatches.

Natural Fiber Fabric Club, 521 Fifth Ave., New York, NY 10175. 100% wools, cottons, silks, and linens at 20% savings over regular retail. Membership, $10/year for four swatched mailings and basic 24-fabric portfolio.

Oppenheim's, Dept. 394, N. Manchester, IN 46962, 219/982-6848. Classic fashion fabrics at a savings. Swatches, $2*. Free swatch mailing after first order.

Portfolio Fabrics, 4984 Manor St., Vancouver, BC V5R 3Y2, Canada. Bimonthly portfolios of imported fine fabric swatches. SASE#.

Samuel Lehrer & Co., 7 Depinedo Ave., Stamford, CT 06902. Fine clothing fabrics, primarily menswear. Swatch kit of over 50 samples, $9.95.

Seventh Avenue Designer Fabric Club, 701 Seventh Ave., Ste. 900, New York, NY 10036. Fabric selections from top-name Seventh Avenue designers at discount prices. Membership, $10/year for four swatched mailings.

Sew Easy Textiles & Trims, P.O. Box 54, Hudson Bay, SK S0E 0Y0, Canada, 306/865-3343. Quality fabrics, low prices. Volume discounts. Notions and patterns. $5# w/swatches.

South Sea Curios, Box 3927, Pago Pago, American Samoa 96799. Pacific Island prints and Polynesian motifs in 100% cotton and blends. Swatches, $4 ($2*).

Southern Fabrics by Mail, 1210 Galleria Mall, Houston, TX 77056, 713/626-5511. Large selection of exclusive imports and designer fabrics at reasonable prices. Membership, $15/year for four swatched mailings.

Southwest Design, 1356 County Road 128, Dept. UN, Hesperus, CO 81326, 303/588-3337. "Practical fabrics for less," including uniform fabrics, satin, lingerie tricot, and matching laces. Send $1* and L-SASE#.

Stitches and Stuff, 1212 72nd Ave. N., Minneapolis, MN 55430. Large selection of cottons, silks, polyesters, linens, wools, and blends. $1 and SASE#.

The Stitchin' Post, 161 Elm, P.O. Box 280, Sisters, OR 97759. Cottons and silks; trims. Catalog, $1.

Tanya's Fabrics, 1039 N. Mills Ave., Orlando, FL 32803, 407/896-1581; 800/331-8986. Color-coordinated Moygashel linen, silks, *Ultrasuede®*, and fine cottons. Swatch collection and fabric club membership, $3*.

Thimbleweed, 2975 College Ave., Berkeley, CA 94705. Cottons, silks, and linens. SASE#.

27th Street Fabrics, 2710 Willamette St., Eugene, OR 97405, 503/345-6224. Fine fabrics and notions plus personalized service for your sewing needs. L-SASE#.

Warren of Stafford, 99 Furnace Ave., Stafford Springs, CT 06076, 800/325-9019; in CT, 203/684-2766. Fine yarns and fabrics of cashmere, camel hair, and wool woven in Stafford's own mill. Swatches, $4* per request.

Winston's Fabrics, 8515 Delmar Blvd., St. Louis, MO 63124, 314/432-5005. Fine designer, classic, and bridal fabrics. SASE#.

The Yardage Shop, 423 Main St., Ridgefield, CT 06877, 203/438-6100. *Ultrasuede®*, *Sofrina*, *Lamous II®*, *Suedemark*, silk, linen, and more. $1#; swatches, $8.50.

Real Leathers

Berman Leather, 25 Melcher St., Boston, MA 02210-1599. Catalog and complete sample set, $5*.

C.T. Textiles, 340 E. 57th St., New York, NY 10022, 212/486-1299. Full color range of smooth-grain skins, suede pigskin, metallic leathers and pearlescents. Minimum order. $1 and SASE with color choice for sample.

D'Anton, Rte. 2, Box 159, West Branch, IA 52358, 319/643-2568. Sueded, smooth, and novelty leathers. L-SASE#.

Frank's Leather and Hide, 3075 17th St., San Francisco, CA 94110, 800/622-2220. Full range of leathers at great prices. Complete set of garment swatches, $11; upholstery color cards, $5.00 each (call first to determine which upholstery swatches you need). Minimum orders, $50; this firm prefers ongoing wholesale accounts.

Iowa Pigskin Sales Co., Box 115, Clive, IA 50053. Suede and smooth, full-grain pigskin, in a range of colors. Sample set, $4*.

The Leather Factory, P.O. Box 50429, Ft. Worth, TX 76105, 800/433-3201. Leather skins, lacing, tools, and books. $3*#.

Leather Unlimited Corp., 7155 County Hwy. "B," UN 800, Belgium, WI 53004, 414/994-9464. Leather, tools, kits, belts, and buckles. Minimum order, $30. $2*#.

The Leather Warehouse, 3134 S. Division, Grand Rapids, MI 49508. Complete line of leather and leather-craft products. Free#.

Leo G. Stein, 4314 N. California Ave., Chicago, IL 60618, 800/831-9509. Garment pig suede, cowhide, embossed leather, and exotics. Minimum order, $25; quantity discounts. $3# w/ swatches.

M. Siegel Co., Inc., 120 Pond St., Ashland, MA 01721, 508/881-5200. Large assortment of colored garment leathers. Minimum order, $30; quantity discounts.

Prairie Collection, RR 1, Box 63, Meservey, IA 50457, 515/358-6344. Incredible fishskin leather, among others. Also, remnants available. $3*#w/samples.

Quintessence, 3166 Maple Dr., Ste. 230, Atlanta, GA 30305, 404/264-1759. Exotic skins, leathers, suedes, and metallics—$4#. Hand-painted cotton fabric—free#. Stones, shell, and bead trims—$4#.

Tandy Leather Co., P.O. Box 2934, Ft. Worth, TX 76113. Smooth leathers, suedes, and exotics. Swatches, $2*; $1#.

Leatherlikes: *Ultrasuede®, Ultraleather®,* etc.

✎ **Note:** Most retailers who carry better fabrics also inventory *Ultrasuede®* fabrics (e.g., *Facile®* and *Caress®*), plus other synthetic suedes and leathers. Those included on this list, however, are mail-order specialists and most offer these fabrics at everyday discounts.

Baer Fabrics, 515 E. Market St., Louisville, KY 40202, 800/288-2237; 502/583-5521. Sample set of *Ultrasuede®, Facile®, Caress®,* and *Lamous*, $7.50. $2#.

Clearbrook Woolens, P.O. Box 8, Clearbrook, VA 22624. Inquire about *Ultrasuede®*-brand scraps at special prices. L-SASE#.

Fabrics Unlimited, 5015 Columbia Pike, Arlington, VA 22204, 703/671-0324. Complete *Ultrasuede®* line. L-SASE#.

Field's Fabrics, 1695 44th S.E., Grand Rapids, MI 49508, 616/455-4570. *Ultrasuede®, Facile®, Caress®,* and *Ultraleather®* swatches, $10* (refundable with order).

G Street Fabrics, 11854 Rockville, MD 20852, 301/231-8960; 800/333-9191 (orders only). Sample chart of *Ultrasuede®* and *Ultraleather®,* $10* each.

Mary Jo's, 401 Cox Rd., Gastonia, NC 28054, 800/MARYJOS (800/627-9567). *Ultrasuede®, Facile®,* and some *Caress®* colors, all at discount prices. Call for more information.

Michiko's Creations, P.O. Box 4313, Napa, CA 94558. All shades of *Ultrasuede®, Ultraleather®, Facile®,* and *Caress®.* Ask about discounted remnant pricing. Swatched catalog, $5. L-SASE#.

UltraMouse, Ltd., 3433 Bennington Ct., Birmingham, MI 48010. *Ultrasuede®* scraps, sold by the pound. L-SASE plus $1.50#.

Ultrascraps, P.O. Box 98, Farmington, UT 84025, 801/451-6023. *Ultrasuede®* scraps and accessory patterns. L-SASE#.

The Yardage Shop, 423 Main, Ridgefield, CT 06877, 203/438-6100. Full line of *Ultrasuede®* fabrics and *Ultraleather®.* Also, *Lamous II®, Suedemark,* and *Sofrina.* For 350 swatches of these and assorted other swatches, send $9.50. $1#.

Other Publications by the Authors

Distinctive Serger Gifts and Crafts, Chilton Book Company, 1989. The first book with one-of-a-kind serger projects using ingenious methods and upscale ideas, by Naomi Baker and Tammy Young. (See ordering information for *Innovative Serging,* below.)

Innovative Serging, Chilton Book Company, 1989. State-of-the-art techniques for overlock sewing by Gail Brown and Tammy Young. Order from Open Chain Publishing, P.O. Box 2634, Dept. SSF, Menlo Park, CA 94026, for $16.95 postpaid ($18 postpaid for California residents).

Innovative Sewing, Chilton Book Company, 1990. A guide to the best in creative sewing with a wealth of dressmaking and home decorating techniques, by Gail Brown and Tammy Young. (See ordering information for *Innovative Serging,* above.)

Serger Update Newsletter, 2269 Chestnut #269, Dept. SSF, San Francisco, CA 94123. The only periodical devoted entirely to serging news and techniques. Published monthly—$36 annual subscription. See the special sampler offer on page *ii.*

Sewing Update Newsletter (see address above). Newsletter format with tips and ideas from sewing professionals (sister publication to *Serger Update* Newsletter). Sent every other month— $18 per year.

The following are *Update Newsletter* booklet publications. They are sold by fabric stores, machine dealers, and mail-order sewing supply companies. Or you can order individual titles for $3.95 each from *Update* Newsletters, 2269 Chestnut #269, Dept. SSF, San Francisco, CA 94123.

Advanced Serging Techniques, by Naomi Baker, 1988. Never-before-published serger techniques applicable to garment, craft, and decorating projects—serged-scalloped edging, serging padded paper, lace over fishing line and wire, three-dimensional flat and padded appliqué, plus double-rolled-edge braid.

Beyond Finishing: Innovative Serging, by Naomi Baker, 1988. A concise, up-to-the-minute report on decorative serging—serged lace, fishline ruffles, tucked and rolled edges, and much more.

Serged Gifts, in Minutes! by Tammy Young, 1988. Charming projects that can be made in an hour or less—like a ruffled hanger, upholstered basket, and firewood carrier (nine total). No pattern purchases are required.

Serging Lingerie, by Naomi Baker, 1988. Learn to serge luxurious lingerie out of both knits and wovens. Edge-finishing and seaming are so easy you can create beautiful basics or trousseau treasures quickly.

Serging Sweaters, by Naomi Baker, 1988. How to select the right fabrics, make your own pattern from a ready-made favorite, plus tips for cutting, seaming, and finishing.

Index